atlanta

Recipes for Entertaining from Atlanta's Top Chefs

cooks

at home

atlanta

Recipes for Entertaining from Atlanta's Top Chefs

cooks

at home

MELISSA LIBBY

FOOD PHOTOGRAPHY BY JOEY IVANSCO
CHEF PHOTOGRAPHY BY TIM WILKERSON

CITYBOOKS
PUBLISHING

MIRAMAR BEACH, FLORIDA

This book is dedicated to my parents, Pat and Pete Libby,
with gratitude for making me believe I could do anything if I tried.

CITYBOOKS
PUBLISHING

Published by
CityBooks Publishing, LLC
PO Box 6541
Miramar Beach, Florida 32550

Printed in China

1st printing 2006

ISBN-13: 978-0-9786609-0-1
ISBN-10: 0-9786609-0-0

A special thanks to Fuji Photo Film Inc. USA's Professional Imaging Division
for the use of its FinePix S-3 digital camera which was used for the food photography.

Jacket and book design by Burtch Hunter Design

A portion of the proceeds from the sale of *Atlanta Cooks at Home* will be donated to these non-profit organizations chosen by the chefs.

JOE AHN
Atlanta Humane Society

MARK ALBA
Atlanta's Table

TODD ANNIS
Atlanta's Table

JOËL ANTUNES
Share Our Strength

RAY BARATA
St. Jude Children's Research Hospital

SHERI DAVIS
Children's Healthcare of Atlanta

SHAUN DOTY
Slow Food USA

DEAN DUPUIS
Atlanta's Table

RON EYESTER
Hospice Atlanta

ELISA GAMBINO
The Bridge

CARVEL GRANT GOULD
American Diabetes Association

LINDA HARRELL
American Cancer Society

DAVID HARTSHORN
ALS Association/Lou Gehrig's Disease

JASON HILL
Cystic Fibrosis Foundation

JUSTIN KEITH
American Red Cross

GERRY KLASKALA
Share Our Strength

NICK OLTARSH
Project Open Hand

SCOTT PEACOCK
Plymouth Harbor Day Program for Older Adults

JOSHUA PERKINS
The Children's School

BARB PIRES
Down Syndrome Association of Atlanta

PIERO PREMOLI
Share Our Strength

BUTCH RAPHAEL
The Bridge

KEVIN RATHBUN
American Lung Association

CRAIG RICHARDS
Atlanta's Table

ANTHONY SANDERS
Atlanta's Table

JAY SWIFT
Atlanta Humane Society

MICHAEL TUOHY
Georgia Organics

VIRGINIA WILLIS
Susan G. Komen Breast Cancer Foundation

MICAH WILLIX
Atlanta's Table

What fun we've had putting *Atlanta Cooks at Home* together! Few people realize how many moving parts are involved to produce a book, especially a cookbook. It starts with the chefs who gave their time and creativity to craft a menu and write the recipes and I thank them all from the bottom of my heart. And then the recipes—all 150+ of them—had to be tested to be sure that the home cook could be successful with them.

Gena Berry led a team of professionals who shopped, cooked, called chefs with questions, and cooked some more. The recipes were also sent to John David Harmon of Whole Foods Market so he could choose the perfect beverage to accompany each meal.

While they were testing and pairing, photographer Joey Ivansco and food stylist Sara Levy were making sure all the food photos were perfect. Between the two of them, no angle was untried, no stray arugula was photographed, no herbs drooped from the heat. Meanwhile, photographer Tim Wilkerson was working with much more animated subject matter—the chefs themselves, along with their families, pets and sports equipment.

To find out more about each chef, members of my staff took to the streets like reporters, interviewing them and writing the copy—on deadline, of course. Next, Rebecca Lang took on the laborious job of proofreading, editing, and indexing everything in the book. Designer Burtch Hunter was the recipient of all these photos and words and once again, he has created a beautiful book.

And then our team at CityBooks Publishing—Kristin Hutchins, Christine Miller, Gina Morris, Greg Vaughan and Sharon McNamara—made our dream a reality. A toast to every single person who contributed to this book and the friends who cheered them on!

Front row, seated: food stylist Sara Levy, designer Burtch Hunter, chief recipe tester Gena Berry.
Back row: recipe tester Vanessa Parker McIntyre, copywriters Meryl Bryant, McCall Mastroianni, Dave Payne, and Marissa Jennings, recipe testers Steffi Stephens, Alison Berry, Lenada Merrick, Teri Grooms, Jason Brooks, Gloria Smiley and Nancy Waldeck. Not pictured: recipe tester Bree Williams.

INTRODUCTION

Five years ago we put together *Atlanta Cooks* to showcase the immense culinary talent in Atlanta restaurants and give readers a chance to create favorite dishes from some of these popular dining spots. With *Atlanta Cooks at Home* we have asked top chefs for their approach to home-based entertaining, sharing their food genius to make meals at your home more delicious and memorable.

Home is the nucleus of our very busy worlds, a place where we gather with family and friends to celebrate a holiday or an accomplishment, share the stories of our lives, or just have fun. There are many reasons to invite people into our homes, but no matter the occasion, good food and drink are essential.

Atlanta Cooks at Home gives you inspired menus for thirty occasions, from the formal to casual, all crafted by the best chefs in the city and expertly paired with beverage suggestions. We also get a peek inside the life of each chef, the men and women we all admire who seem larger than life. It's fun to be reminded that they have families, pets, dreams and wishes, just like we all do.

Chefs may entertain hundreds every day, but in *Atlanta Cooks at Home* we see they can also throw a great dinner party for six. It is our hope that this book can be a resource for your next gathering.

HERE'S TO GREAT COOKING AT HOME!

A special thanks to John David Harmon of Whole Foods Market for pairing drinks with every menu. He enthusiastically read each recipe looking for definitive flavors in order to select the appropriate beverages to accompany the menu. His suggestions are broad and timeless, the sort of information you would get from the wine guy at your favorite store. In fact, he is that wine guy.

Harmon, specialty coordinator for wine and cheese for Whole Foods Market's South Region, started his connection with food and wine early in life. His father was a chef and a stickler for quality ingredients, and gave John David his first job...putting bread on plates for a dollar per night. The family always toasted the new year with real French Champagne and he has been hooked on sparkling wine ever since. In fact, he often says he would sell his house and move to France for the opportunity to make Champagne.

After attending the University of Georgia, John David moved to Spain where he would make frequent trips out into the wine country, staying in an old farmhouse to be closer to the different wineries and to get to know the winemakers themselves. John David could truly taste the differences in all of the wines, and he remembers thinking, "Wow! There is so much to this, and I want to learn it all!" After this experience, John David began writing a monthly wine column for *Barcelona Metropolitan*.

Feeling the need to continue his education and training, John David went back to school to earn his MBA-IM. From there he moved to La Paz, Bolivia and worked as a consultant while honing his now fluent Spanish. However, he couldn't get wine and cheese out of his head, so he returned to Atlanta and worked as a cheese monger and buyer for Star Provisions.

It was from this job that he eventually moved to Whole Foods Market, where he says he has found a home. "Whole Foods Market allows you to blaze your own trail," he said. "The freedom that the company gives to pursue groundbreaking avenues is incredible. Not to mention an endless supply of new wines, beers, cheeses and chocolates to explore."

SHAUN DOTY

{ SHAUN'S }

Dinner Under the Tuscan Sun

Spanish Style Gazpacho

Fava Beans and Pecorino Toscano

Watermelon and Goat Cheese Salad

Panzanella Tuscan Tomato and Bread Salad

Risi e Bisi (Risotto with Fresh Peas)

Spanish Style Gazpacho

{ Serves 4 }

1½ pounds tomatoes (about 5 large)
1½ cups cucumber, seeded and roughly chopped (2 small cucumbers)
3 leaves fresh basil
¼ cup roughly chopped shallot (1 large)
1 teaspoon garlic, roughly chopped
1 tablespoon plus 1½ teaspoons sherry vinegar
½ cup water, plus more if necessary
½ cup fresh bread cubes
½ cup extra virgin olive oil
Kosher or sea salt and freshly ground pepper to taste

~

In a 6-quart stock pot, bring 4 quarts of water to a boil. With a paring knife, cut a shallow "X" in the bottom of each tomato. Once the water is boiling, drop the tomatoes in a few at a time, and leave for 15-30 seconds or until you see the skin begin to split. Remove the tomatoes from the boiling water and drop into a large bowl of ice water to stop the cooking.

Once the tomatoes are cool, pull the skin off with the tip of your knife. Once all the skins are removed, roughly chop the tomatoes.

Place the tomatoes in a blender and add the cucumber, basil, shallot, garlic, vinegar, and water. Blend until smooth. Add the bread cubes and pulse 5 more times. While the blender is running, slowly stream in the olive oil. If the soup seems too thick, add a little water. Season with salt and pepper and serve chilled.

Fava Beans with Pecorino Toscano

{ Serves 4 to 6 }

2-2½ pounds fresh fava beans (2 cups shelled)
3 tablespoons red wine vinegar
¼ cup minced shallots (1 large)
¼ cup extra virgin olive oil
½ cup diced tomato (1 medium)
¼ cup loosely packed, minced fresh mint leaves
4 ounces Pecorino Toscano cheese, diced into ¼-inch cubes
Salt and freshly ground pepper to taste

~

Remove the fava beans from the pods by breaking open each pod and dislodging the beans.

In a 6-quart stock pot, bring 3 quarts of water to a boil. Drop the beans in the water and cook for 2-3 minutes. Drain the beans and run under cold water to stop the cooking. Once the beans are cool, peel the outer skin from each bean. Cover and chill.

In a medium mixing bowl, combine the red wine vinegar and shallots. Whisking constantly, slowly drizzle in the olive oil until the mixture is emulsified. Add the tomato, mint, cheese, and chilled fava beans. Season with salt and pepper. Toss well to combine then serve on chilled plates.

"A lot of my friends were going to work for the big restaurant companies that were emerging—like Brinker. I wanted to do something more creative. I moved to Dallas and worked in a bistro. I knew that was for me."

Watermelon and Goat Cheese Salad

{ Serves 6 }

4 cups watermelon balls
¼ teaspoon kosher salt
¼ cup extra virgin olive oil
¼ cup saba*
3 ounces Sweet Grass Dairy fresh goat cheese
5 fresh basil leaves, torn into small pieces

~

In a medium bowl, toss watermelon balls, salt, olive oil and saba. Toss lightly just to mix. Cover bowl with plastic wrap and refrigerate until serving time.

Divide watermelon onto 6 chilled plates. Crumble goat cheese on top and sprinkle with basil.

*Saba is a slightly sweet, unfermented syrup made from the must of Trebbiano grapes, the same grapes that balsamic vinegar is made from, and is actually a by-product of balsamic vinegar. It is widely used in Italy in sweet and savory cooking. It can be found in specialty food stores.

"One day, I would love to buy a farm and do a culinary program there. Something I would find very interesting and could share with people."

Panzanella Tuscan Tomato and Bread Salad

{ Serves 4 }

3 tablespoons red wine vinegar
¼ cup minced shallots (1 large)
¼ cup extra virgin olive oil
1½ pounds heirloom tomatoes, (4-5 large) seeded and cut into ½-inch wedges
1 cup peeled, seeded, and diced cucumber (1 small)
6 ounces stale French bread cut into ½-inch cubes (about 2 cups)*
6 basil leaves, torn
Salt and freshly ground pepper
4 white anchovy filets

~

In a large mixing bowl combine the vinegar and shallots. Using a whisk slowly drizzle in the olive oil in a constant steady stream until the mixture is emulsified. Add the tomatoes, cucumber, bread and basil. Toss gently to combine and season with salt and pepper. Serve immediately on chilled plates, garnishing each salad with 1 anchovy filet.

*If you don't have stale bread put the bread cubes on a baking sheet in a preheated 250° oven for 10 minutes or until the bread is crunchy.

Risi e Bisi

RISOTTO WITH FRESH PEAS

{ Serves 6 }

6 pounds fresh English peas, shelled, about 2½ cups
¼ cup plus 2 tablespoons olive oil
6 cups unsalted chicken stock
2 cups Arborio or risotto style rice
¼ cup minced shallots (1 large)
4 tablespoons unsalted butter (½ stick)
½ cup grated Parmigiano-Reggiano cheese
Salt and freshly ground pepper

~

In a 6-quart stock pot, bring 3 quarts of water to a boil. Drop the peas in the boiling water and cook for 1-2 minutes, or until crisp tender. Drain the peas and put into a bowl of ice water to stop the cooking. Once the peas have cooled, drain. In a food processor or blender, put ½ cup of the peas and 2 tablespoons of olive oil and purée until very smooth; set aside.

In a 2-3-quart saucepan, heat the chicken stock over medium-low heat. In a Dutch oven, heat the remaining ¼ cup of olive oil over medium heat. Add the rice and shallots and sauté for 3-4 minutes or until the shallots are soft. Stir the hot chicken stock into the rice and shallot mixture in 1-cup increments, allowing each cup to be absorbed before adding the next.

When almost all of the stock is used, taste for doneness. The Arborio should be creamy with just a little bite after about 20 minutes. Add the butter, cheese, and pea puree. Fold in the remaining peas, season with salt and pepper and serve.

WHAT TO DRINK

These light treats will pair nicely with a light, fruity Italian Pinot Grigio. Alternatively, try out Tuscany's classic white wine, Vernaccia di San Gimignano.

SHAUN DOTY

has put his culinary fingerprint on a number of great Atlanta restaurants over the years, including MidCity Cuisine, Mumbo Jumbo and Table 1280. With Shaun's he continues the journey, serving up fresh seasonal ingredients, simply and creatively. A high school guidance counselor persuaded Shaun that a career in hotels or restaurants seemed more suitable to his background than his goal of becoming an optometrist. He studied hospitality management at Oklahoma State University and then culinary arts at Johnson & Wales University in Charleston, SC.

Finish the sentence, "I wish I could..."
Have more hours in a day.

What did you want to be when you grew up?
An optometrist. It sounded cool.

In high school, you were voted most likely to....
Never graduate.

What's your most used quote in the kitchen?
"Service!"

What's your favorite dish to prepare?
I like improv. It's fun to just make something up with whatever I have.

What's your favorite TV show?
The Sopranos.

What's the strangest food you've ever consumed?
I ate freshwater seaweed in Tokyo. Apparently it is considered a delicacy. That eluded me.

What movie can you watch over and over?
The Godfather.

If you won the lottery, what would you do with the money?
Buy an island and staff if with bikini chicks! I'd also set up college scholarships for my nieces and nephews. A Gulfstream would be cool too.

BUTCH RAPHAEL

PANGAEA

International Brunch

Middle Eastern Breakfast

Cucumber and Tomato Salad

Sumac-Marinated Onions

Hummus

Strawberry and Cream Cheese Stuffed French Toast

Mango and Coconut Pancakes

Middle Eastern Breakfast

{ Serves 4 to 6 }

4 malawa or paratha or roti (Middle Eastern flatbread)
Tomato Sauce
8 eggs, cooked to order (fried eggs look great on this plate)
Hummus
Cucumber and Tomato Salad
Sumac-Marinated Onions
½ cup whole, pitted kalamata olives
4 ounces feta cheese, diced

~

Pan fry the flatbread until puffed and starting to brown. Place the flatbread on plate, top with tomato sauce and cooked eggs. Garnish the plate with a scoop of hummus, cucumber and tomato salad, sumac-marinated onions, olives and diced feta cheese.

TOMATO SAUCE

2 tablespoons olive oil
1¼ cup yellow onion, diced (1 medium onion)
1½ teaspoons minced garlic (1 clove)
1 tablespoon dried oregano
2 teaspoons dried basil
1 16-ounce can diced tomatoes
1 8-ounce can tomato sauce
1 teaspoon kosher salt

~

Heat a medium, straight-sided, non-reactive (stainless is fine) sauté pan over medium heat. Add oil and swirl to cover bottom of pan. When oil is heated, add onion and garlic and sweat until fragrant and soft, about 5 minutes. Add oregano, basil, diced tomatoes with juice and tomato sauce. Bring to a simmer, reduce heat and cook one hour.

Raphael always knew he wanted to cook. He asked for a wok for his 13th birthday. "It was a great escape from doing homework."

Hummus

1 16-ounce can garbanzo beans, drained and rinsed
2 teaspoons minced garlic
¼ cup tahini (sesame paste)
½ teaspoon paprika
3 tablespoons freshly squeezed lemon juice
½ teaspoon salt
¼ cup water
1 teaspoon lemon zest

~

In the bowl of a food processor fitted with a steel blade, blend beans, garlic, tahini, paprika, lemon juice and salt. With processor running, add water, just until hummus is spreadable. Stir in lemon zest, taste and adjust seasoning as needed.
Chill before serving.

Cucumber and Tomato Salad

2 cucumbers
1 tomato, seeded and diced
3 tablespoons extra virgin olive oil
2 tablespoons freshly squeezed lemon juice
½ teaspoon minced garlic
½ teaspoon kosher salt
1 pinch freshly ground pepper

~

With a spoon, remove seeds from cucumber, dice into ½-inch pieces. Cut tomato in half and remove seeds, dice into ½-inch pieces. Mix the cucumber and tomato in a large mixing bowl. Toss in olive oil, lemon juice, garlic, salt and pepper. Cover and let sit for at least 1 hour prior to serving.

Sumac-Marinated Onions

2 tablespoons freshly squeezed lemon juice
1 tablespoon extra virgin olive oil
2 teaspoons ground sumac (found at specialty groceries and international markets)
½ teaspoon kosher salt
1 red onion, thiny sliced

~

Mix lemon juice, olive oil, sumac and salt and stir until well combined. Add onion. Let marinate at least 1 hour before serving. These will hold in refrigerator for up to 1 week and actually get better with age.

An avid traveler, Raphael hopes to one day make it back to Vietnam where he was born. Asked to describe his favorite vacation spot Raphael says, "anywhere . . . a vacation would be great!"

Strawberry and Cream Cheese Stuffed French Toast

{ Serves 4 }

6 large eggs, lightly beaten
¼ cup milk
⅛ teaspoon ground cinnamon
8 ounces cream cheese, cut into 8 slices and brought to room temperature
8 slices challah (egg bread)
1 pint fresh strawberries, thinly sliced
2 tablespoons unsalted butter
Maple syrup or honey for serving

~

In a large flat bowl or pie plate, lightly beat the eggs with milk. Stir in cinnamon. Spread the cream cheese slices evenly on one side of each challah slice. Divide the strawberries between 4 pieces of bread and top with remaining 4 pieces of bread, making cream cheese and strawberry sandwiches. Dip each sandwich in the egg mixture, letting the custard soak into the bread.

Heat a large sauté pan or griddle over medium heat. Brush griddle with a generous amount of butter and heat until the foam subsides. Pan fry the French toast over medium heat until golden brown, about 5 minutes. If the bread browns too fast, reduce heat. Gently turn and cook until golden brown on second side, another 5 minutes. Serve hot with maple syrup or honey.

Mango and Coconut Pancakes

{ Serves 4 }

3 mangos, diced
1 cup shredded fresh coconut (if using dried coconut, use unsweetened)
¾ cup milk
3 tablespoons unsalted butter, melted, divided
1 large egg, lightly beaten
1 cup all-purpose flour
2 teaspoons baking powder
2 tablespoons sugar
½ teaspoon salt

~

Remove seed from the mango and cut into ½-inch dice. In a large mixing bowl mix mango, coconut, milk, 2 tablespoons melted butter and egg. Stir the dry ingredients together and gently stir into the mango and milk mixture to make the pancake batter, leaving a few lumps. If the mixture seems a bit dry, add a little milk to thin it to batter consistency.

Heat a large sauté pan or griddle over medium heat. Spread remaining 1 tablespoon butter on the griddle and drop the pancake batter on the grill with a ⅓-cup measuring cup or ladle. Batter should spread, begin to bubble and steam and begin to dry on top. When the steaming has stopped, pancake should be a light golden brown; turn and cook until cooked through, about 3 minutes per side.

WHAT TO DRINK

You can't beat a pitcher of freshly squeezed orange juice and a pot of coffee for this wonderful breakfast menu.

BUTCH RAPHAEL

makes it clear, that to him, family is everything. He credits his family with providing the most inspiration and support for his successful career. Even with his international taste, Raphael, owner of Pangaea, says that his favorite thing to eat when he isn't at his restaurant is anyone else's home cooking. "People shouldn't be afraid to cook, home cooking is good."

What's the oddest food you've ever eaten?
Mustard and black pepper sandwiches? I guess some people might think that's odd.

What's your favorite time of day?
Sunday mornings when all the kids pile in the bed with me and their mom. Or equally, at night when all the kids are in bed and we can have some time to ourselves!

If you could have a different job for a day, what would it be?
Probably a diving guide in Bali or the Maltese Islands.

What's your favorite book?
The Power of One by Bryce Courtenay.

What's your favorite dish to prepare?
I love to cook anything but probably my favorite thing to cook is breakfast. I never have time though!

What's your favorite guilty pleasure?
Sleep.

If you could cook a meal for anyone who would it be?
I'd like to be able to cook for my grandparents before they passed away.

What's something that people would be surprised to find out about you?
I love to play video games.

RON EYESTER

{ FOOD 101 }

Supper Club

Low Country Shrimp and Grits with Andouille Sausage
and San Marzano Tomato Gravy

Herb Roasted Springer Mountain Chicken
with Mustard Whipped Potatoes and Honey-Thyme Pan Jus

Vanilla and Rosemary Scented Pork Loin
with Smoked Gouda and Cranberry Mac and Cheese

Heirloom Tomatoes with Pineapple, Cilantro
and Sweet Grass Dairy Goat Cheese

Un-Classic Shrimp Bisque with Coconut Milk

Low Country Shrimp and Grits with Andouille Sausage and San Marzano Tomato Gravy

{ Serves 6 }

4 tablespoons unsalted butter, divided
2 cups thinly sliced Vidalia onion (about 2 medium onions)
1½ cups stone ground grits (Logan Turnpike recommended)
1¾ cups half and half
3¼ cups chicken broth, divided
½ teaspoon granulated garlic
½ teaspoon granulated sugar
1 tablespoon finely chopped garlic
1 cup chopped andouille sausage (about ¼ pound)
1 14-ounce can chopped San Marzano tomatoes (Cento brand recommended)
½ pound fresh Georgia shrimp, peeled and deveined
¼ cup finely chopped assorted herbs (oregano, thyme, marjoram and parsley)
Kosher salt and freshly ground pepper

~

In a large, straight sided sauté pan, heat 2 tablespoons butter over medium heat and swirl to coat the bottom of the pan. Add the onions and heat until they are starting to soften, about 5 minutes. Reduce the heat and let the onions cook undisturbed for 20 minutes. If the onions start to brown, give them a quick stir and reduce the heat a little. After 20 minutes, give the onions a stir and continue to cook, stirring only occasionally, until the onions have caramelized (turned very soft, light golden brown and sweet).

In a large saucepan, bring half and half and 2 cups chicken broth to a boil. Gradually whisk in grits and return to a boil. Reduce heat to a simmer and cook grits about 30 minutes over low heat, stirring often to prevent scorching. If the grits become too thick, add a little half and half or broth. When the grits are done, they will be soft and creamy with just a little "bite." Season the grits with the granulated garlic, a pinch of sugar, and salt and pepper to taste.

While the grits are cooking, add the garlic to the caramelized onions and increase the heat to medium-high. Cook until the garlic is fragrant, about 1 minute. Scrape the onion mixture to the side of the pan and add the sausage. Let the sausage cook for an additional 5-7 minutes, turning to brown on both sides. Add the tomatoes and chicken broth and bring to a boil. Reduce the heat to a simmer and let the mixture reduce and thicken, about 10 minutes. Add the shrimp; cook just until curled and opaque, about 4 minutes. Stir in the remaining 2 tablespoons butter, herbs, and salt and pepper to taste.

"My favorite dish to cook is shrimp and grits. I think it defines who I am. I learned how to cook in Charleston; it was where I was when I made the turn in my career from just a job to a passion."

Herb Roasted Springer Mountain Chicken with Mustard Whipped Potatoes and Honey-Thyme Pan Jus

{ Serves 2 to 4 }

2 cups honey, divided
1 cup fresh herbs such as thyme, oregano, rosemary and parsley, chopped
¼ cup minced garlic
3 tablespoons extra virgin olive oil
2 tablespoons fresh lemon juice plus more for finishing the sauce
1 3- to 4-pound organic chicken, preferably Springer Mountain Farms
Kosher salt and freshly ground pepper
3 Russet potatoes, peeled and cubed
½ pound (2 sticks) unsalted butter, divided
½ cup whole grain mustard
¾ cup whole milk
Dash white truffle oil
2 cups chicken stock
2 sprigs fresh thyme

~

In a large bowl, combine 1 cup of the honey, herbs, garlic, olive oil and lemon juice. Add the chicken and turn to coat. Cover loosely with plastic wrap and refrigerate to marinate at least 2 hours.

Preheat oven to 300°. Remove chicken from the refrigerator about 30 minutes before roasting. Place rack in roasting pan. Season chicken with salt and pepper. Place chicken on rack and roast for 1 hour and 25 minutes. Increase temperature to 375° and bake for an additional 20 minutes or until the juices run clear when the thigh is pierced and a meat thermometer reaches 160°.

While the chicken is cooking, place the potatoes in a saucepan and cover with cold water. Bring to a boil and reduce the heat to simmer. Cook the potatoes until fork tender, about 25 minutes. Remove from the heat and pour into a colander to drain. Place potatoes back in the warm pot to evaporate any excess moisture. Add 1 stick of butter, mustard, milk and truffle oil. Season with salt and pepper. Beat with a handheld mixer until light, fluffy and well combined. Keep warm.

Remove chicken from the oven and transfer the chicken to a cutting board. Let rest for about 15 minutes; reserve roasting pan and drippings.

While the chicken is resting, cut the remaining stick of butter into cubes and set aside. In a small saucepan, combine the pan drippings, chicken stock and thyme and place over medium-high heat. Bring to a boil and reduce heat to a simmer. Cook until slightly reduced, about 8 minutes. Add remaining cup of honey and a squeeze of lemon juice. Taste and adjust seasoning with salt and pepper. Stir until well combined. Remove the thyme sprigs and discard. Remove from the heat and whisk in remaining butter.

To serve, divide potatoes between 4 warm plates and top with sliced chicken. Spoon over jus and serve immediately.

Vanilla and Rosemary Scented Pork Loin with Smoked Gouda and Cranberry Mac and Cheese

{ Serves 6 }

½ cup maple syrup
½ cup apple cider
½ cup finely chopped fresh rosemary
2 vanilla beans, split and scraped
1 tablespoon minced garlic
2 teaspoons ground cumin
1 4- to 5-pound center-cut pork loin
Kosher salt and freshly ground pepper
Smoked Gouda and Cranberry Mac and Cheese

~

Combine maple syrup, apple cider, rosemary, vanilla, garlic and cumin in a large bowl. Add pork and turn to coat. Cover loosely with plastic wrap and refrigerate to marinate at least 3 hours.

Preheat oven to 325°. Remove pork from the refrigerator about 30 minutes before roasting. Place rack in roasting pan. Season roast on all sides with salt and pepper. Place pork on rack and roast in oven until thermometer inserted in center of pork registers 150°, 45 minutes to 1 hour. The pork will be slightly pink in the center. Remove the roasting pan from the oven and let the pork rest on a warm platter covered with foil for 10-15 minutes. While the meat is resting, the internal temperature of the roast will rise to at least 155° because of carryover cooking.

"I wish I could make everyone understand why I feel the way I do about cooking. It isn't just a job—it is a lifestyle; you take it home with you."

SMOKED GOUDA AND CRANBERRY MAC AND CHEESE

{ Serves 6 }

1 tablespoon unsalted butter, room temperature
1½ cups heavy cream
½ teaspoon freshly grated nutmeg
1½ cups smoked Gouda, skin removed and coarsely grated
2 cups dried elbow macaroni, preferably Barilla, cooked al denté
¾ cup dried cranberries, reconstituted and drained
½ cup panko (Japanese breadcrumbs)
Kosher salt and freshly ground pepper

~

Preheat oven to 375°. Brush a 2½-quart deep round or square baking dish with butter and set aside.

Combine heavy cream and nutmeg in a large saucepan. Bring to a boil over medium-high heat, reduce heat and simmer for 5 minutes or until the cream begins to thicken. Watch the pot as it will easily boil over. When the cream mixture has reduced by about one-third, stir in 1 cup of cheese, the pasta and drained cranberries. Season with salt and pepper to taste.

Transfer the macaroni mixture to the prepared baking dish. Top with panko and remaining ½ cup cheese. Bake until hot, bubbly and golden brown, about 20 minutes.

Heirloom Tomatoes with Pineapple, Cilantro and Sweet Grass Dairy Goat Cheese

{ Serves 4 }

3 heirloom or vine-ripe tomatoes, cored and sliced into ¼-inch slices
1 fresh very ripe pineapple, peeled, cored and sliced into ¼-inch slices
2 tablespoons extra virgin olive oil
1 tablespoon freshly squeezed lemon juice
¼ cup chopped cilantro
Sea salt and freshly ground pepper
1 cup Sweet Grass Dairy goat cheese

~

Alternately arrange tomatoes and pineapple on an oval platter. Drizzle with olive oil and lemon juice. Season with salt and pepper. Garnish with chopped cilantro and goat cheese.

Un-Classic Shrimp Bisque with Coconut Milk

{ Serves 8 }

8 tablespoons chilled unsalted butter, cut into tablespoons
1 cup diced celery
1 cup diced onion
1 cup diced carrot
1 tablespoon freshly grated ginger
5 cups chicken or vegetable stock
1 cup canned crushed tomatoes, preferably San Marzano
⅓ cup Mae Ploy sweet chili sauce

1 pound cooked small shrimp, peeled and deveined, divided
½ teaspoon ground cardamom
½ teaspoon ground cloves
½ teaspoon ground cinnamon
1 cup tomato paste, preferably San Marzano
1 14-ounce can unsweetened coconut milk
Kosher salt and freshly ground pepper
Fresh cilantro

Heat a large saucepan over medium heat. Add 1 tablespoon butter and swirl pan to melt. When the butter is melted, add the celery, onions and carrots. Cook, stirring constantly, until they begin to caramelize, about 5-6 minutes. Add the ginger and continue to cook. Add stock, tomatoes and chili sauce. Reduce heat slightly and continue to simmer for 20 minutes.

Add three-fourths of the shrimp, cardamom, cloves and cinnamon to the stock mixture and stir to combine. Add the tomato paste and purée until smooth with a handheld immersion blender. Strain the mixture through a fine mesh sieve.

Place the strained mixture back in the pot and purée again, gradually adding the remaining 7 tablespoons of butter, piece by piece, blending until velvety smooth. Stir in the coconut milk. Taste and season with salt and pepper as needed. Ladle into individual serving bowls and garnish with remaining shrimp and chopped cilantro.

WHAT TO DRINK

For exotic and tropical flavors you must turn to the world's most versatile white wine, Riesling. Try out a German Riesling from one of the magnificent recent vintages to go with the first two courses. Splurge on a premium California Chardonnay that can stand up to the shrimp and grits as well as the chicken. Open up a voluptuous Merlot for the pork. The wine's ripe fruit is tamed only by the vanilla and woodsy flavors fostered during the barrel aging.

didn't always know he wanted to be a chef. "When I was a kid I wanted to be a soldier. It wasn't until I had my first job when I was 16 at the Watermill Inn on Long Island—I was a busboy—that I knew I was supposed to be in the kitchen." While learning to cook in kitchens along the East coast, Eyester also experimented with jobs as a plumbing apprentice, legal assistant, English teacher and advertising sales rep. He explains that his approach to work and life is that "everyone is family. I treat everyone the same at the restaurant and at home. I love to entertain—to take care of people."

Who's the most famous person you've ever cooked for?
Jack Nicklaus at the Masters in Augusta, Georgia.

If you could have another job for a day, what would it be?
I'd be a truck driver—I love to drive.

What are four movies you could watch over and over?
Almost Famous, The Karate Kid, The Italian Job and *Ocean's Eleven*.

What's the funniest thing that has happened to you on the job site?
One time I was working a station and the chef said he was going to get something from the cooler. Next thing we knew, he'd left— he went to the cooler for one thing and just never came back.

If you could have a theme song playing every time you walk into the kitchen, what would it be?
"You Enjoy Myself" by Phish. I'm a huge Phish fan.

What was your favorite trip?
For our honeymoon, my wife and I drove cross-country and we stopped all along the way to eat at all the restaurants we'd always wanted to visit.

CARVEL GRANT GOULD

{ CANOE }

Bridal or Baby Shower

Crispy Plantain, Orange and Avocado Salad

Seared Shrimp with Fresh Peas and Applewood Smoked Bacon

The Perfect Shower Chicken Salad

Roasted Georgia Peaches Stuffed
with Walnut Brown Sugar and Crème Frâiche

Watermelon Mojito

Crispy Plantain, Orange and Avocado Salad

{ Serves 6 to 8 }

6 oranges
⅓ cup fine quality sherry vinegar
1 cup Arberquina or other fine Spanish olive oil
¼ cup finely minced shallots
1 teaspoon sea salt
Coarsely ground black pepper
3 firm green plantains, thinly sliced lengthwise on a mandoline
Canola oil for frying
1 small red onion, thinly sliced on a mandoline
2 ripe avocados, diced
8 ounces mixed greens

~

Juice 2 oranges, segment remaining 4 and reserve for later use.

In a small bowl, mix the orange juice, vinegar, olive oil, shallots, salt and pepper and whisk to combine. Set aside.

Heat a large heavy-bottom pan filled with 3 inches of canola oil over medium-high heat to 300°. Fry the plantains in batches until golden brown and crispy, about 3-5 minutes depending on slice width. Remove with a slotted spoon to a paper towel lined plate to drain. Sprinkle with salt. Let plantains cool to room temperature and crumble.

In a large bowl, toss the orange segments, onion, and avocado. Whisk the vinaigrette and add ¼ cup vinaigrette to the orange mixture. Season with salt and pepper and gently toss to combine.

In a separate bowl, toss the greens with just enough dressing to lightly coat the leaves.

To serve, place a bed of salad on each plate. Top with the orange mixture and garnish with the crumbled plantains.

"I love gardening, especially planting flowers. I have numerous flower beds around my house and I try to make sure each room in my house has fresh flowers."

Seared Shrimp with Fresh Peas and Applewood Smoked Bacon

8 slices applewood smoked bacon, diced
20 large fresh Georgia shrimp, peeled and deveined
1 cup fresh lady peas
1 cup English peas
1 cup fresh corn (3 ears)
1 teaspoon minced garlic
¼ cup minced shallot (about 2 small)
⅓ cup finely chopped Italian parsley
¼ cup Dijon mustard
2 tablespoons apple cider vinegar
½ cup extra virgin olive oil
¼ cup fresh tarragon, chiffonade
Kosher salt and freshly ground pepper
1 cup grape tomatoes, halved

~

Render bacon in large sauté pan until crispy. Remove bacon to a paper towel lined plate. Reserve pan and drippings. Season both sides of shrimp with salt and pepper. Heat the sauté pan and pour out all but about 1 tablespoon of the bacon fat. Add the shrimp and cook until pink and curled, about 2 minutes; turn over and cook until opaque, another 1-2 minutes. Remove the shrimp to a plate to cool.

Fill a large saucepan three-fourths full with water. Add 1 tablespoon salt and bring to a boil. Blanch the peas and corn by immersing for 4 minutes in the boiling water and removing with a sieve or slotted spoon to an ice bath and then to a colander. Work in batches as necessary. Bring the water to a boil before adding a new batch of vegetables.

In a large bowl, whisk and combine the garlic, shallots, parsley, mustard, vinegar, olive oil and tarragon. Season to taste with salt and pepper. Fold in the shrimp, bacon, peas, corn and grape tomatoes just until combined. Serve at room temperature.

The Perfect Shower Chicken Salad

{ Serves 8 }

½ cup freshly squeezed lemon juice
½ teaspoon paprika
2 teaspoons fresh black pepper
2 teaspoons kosher salt
2 tablespoons olive oil
5 skinless boneless chicken breasts
½ cup diced celery (about 4 stalks)
¼ cup finely diced yellow onion (about ½ small onion)
¼ cup finely chopped parsley
⅓ cup sliced almonds, toasted
⅓ cup dried cherries
1¼ cups Hellmann's or Duke's mayonnaise
1 tablespoon curry powder
1 teaspoon celery salt

~

Mix lemon juice, paprika, pepper, salt and olive oil. Place chicken in the mixture to marinate for 30 minutes. Heat a large sauté pan over medium-high heat. Add oil and swirl to coat bottom of pan. Sear the chicken for 3 minutes or until golden brown; turn and cook until the juices run clear and a meat thermometer reaches 165°. Remove to a platter to cool. Cut the cooled chicken into small bite sized pieces and set aside.

In a large bowl, mix the celery, onion, parsley, almonds, dried cherries, mayonnaise, curry powder and celery salt. Stir to combine. Fold in the cooked chicken. Refrigerate until serving.

Carvel taught horseback riding and rode in shows when she was younger.

Roasted Georgia Peaches Stuffed with Walnut Brown Sugar and Crème Frâiche

{ Serves 8 }

2 tablespoons unsalted butter
4 ripe Georgia peaches
2 tablespoons freshly squeezed lemon juice
1 cup firmly packed brown sugar
¼ cup all-purpose flour
½ teaspoon ground cinnamon
¼ teaspoon ground ginger
½ teaspoon salt
3 tablespoons cold unsalted butter, cut into small cubes
¼ cup toasted walnuts, finely chopped
¼ cup rolled oats
¾ cup crème frâiche
⅛ teaspoon freshly grated nutmeg

~

Brush the inside of a 9- x 11-inch baking dish with butter and set aside. Preheat oven to 350°.

Peel the peaches, cut in half, remove the pit and place in a large bowl. Toss with lemon juice and set aside. In a large mixing bowl, combine sugar, flour, cinnamon, ginger and salt. Stir with a whisk to thoroughly mix. Cut in the cubed butter with a pastry cutter or fork until the mixture is coarse and the butter is broken into pea sized pieces. Fold in the walnuts and oats. Place the peach halves cut side up in the prepared baking dish. Spoon the mixture between the peach halves. Bake, uncovered, for 25 minutes or until peaches are soft. Remove from the oven and cool to room temperature.

In a small mixing bowl, mix crème frâiche with nutmeg. To serve, place a peach half on a dessert plate, spoon a dollop of the nutmeg crème frâiche on top of peach and serve.

Watermelon Mojito

{ Serves 4 }

1 medium seedless watermelon
1 cup granulated sugar plus 2 teaspoons for muddling
½ teaspoon salt
4 sprigs mint
¼ cup freshly squeezed lime juice (about 1 lime)
¼ cup chilled simple syrup
¾ cup chilled rum

~

Cut the watermelon into quarters; cut one quarter into ½-inch wedges for garnish and set aside. Remove rind from remaining watermelon and cut the flesh into cubes. Discard the rind. In a blender, combine watermelon, 1 cup sugar and salt and purée until sugar is dissolved. Strain through fine mesh sieve and refrigerate until very cold.

Combine mint sprigs and remaining sugar in a large shaker glass. Using a long teaspoon, "muddle" and bruise the mint to mix and release the flavor and mix. Fill the shaker with crushed ice. Add 1¼ cups watermelon syrup, lime juice, simple syrup and rum. Cover and shake well. Strain into martini glasses. Add a little crushed ice and garnish with the sliced watermelon wedges.

SIMPLE SYRUP

1 cup sugar
1 cup water

~

In a small saucepan, combine sugar and water. Bring to a boil and stir to dissolve sugar. Pour into a glass or metal container and chill.

WHAT TO DRINK

When it comes time to celebrate, look no further than Burgundy's northern most appellation, Chablis. Although this French classic has a name marred by California jug wines, it is simply sublime. Far from overblown and oaky, this Chardonnay exhibits racy acidity, flinty reflection of *terroir*, and the flexibility to match an array of flavors.

CARVEL GRANT GOULD

first became interested in cooking during high school. She kept telling her parents that she wanted to become a chef, which they weren't happy about at all. Her mom got her a job at Buckhead Diner with Gerry Klaskala, figuring she'd become disinterested and forget about it. That was 1989. Always an entrepreneur, Carvel used to go door to door to sell things to her neighbors when she was young. She says she'd pick her neighbor's daffodils and sell them and also sell homemade goods such as chocolate and barrettes.

What TV shows do you watch?
Anything on any of the science channels.

If you could have a theme song playing every time you walk into the kitchen, what would it be?
The theme from *Sanford and Son*. One of the sous chefs is always breaking out into it.

What famous people have you cooked for?
Elizabeth Taylor and Bono of U2. In fact, U2 has rented out Canoe and I remember seeing Bono asleep in one of the booths in Canoe's bar area. He left his jacket there when U2 left and we had to get someone to come pick it up.

What's your guilty pleasure?
Italian shoes.

What's your favorite vacation spot?
Any beach, or anywhere with a breeze and water.

If you could be another occupation for a day, what would it be?
A doctor.

What's your favorite childhood memory?
Riding my Big Wheel. I used to ride down hills and then spin out at the bottom. Of course, I always did this in a dress without shoes. My legs were always scraped up.

MICAH WILLIX

{ ECCO }

Summertime Rendezvous

—

Fried Goat Cheese with Honey and Cracked Pepper

Garlic Shrimp with Olive Oil and Fresh Bay

Roasted Baby Beets with Saba

Fig Glazed Rack of Lamb with Chicory and Warm Potato Salad

Oak Grilled Asparagus with Marinated Tomato Salad

Fried Goat Cheese with Honey and Cracked Pepper

{ Serves 4 to 6 }

8 ounces goat cheese
2 cups all-purpose flour, divided
1 tablespoon kosher salt, divided
1 tablespoon freshly ground pepper, divided, additional for garnish
½ teaspoon baking soda
1 cup chilled club soda
Canola oil for frying
3 tablespoons honey

~

Divide goat cheese into 1-ounce portions. Shape into 1-inch balls. Refrigerate for at least 30 minutes.

Combine 1 cup flour and 2 teaspoons each salt and pepper in a shallow plate to make the seasoned flour. Combine remaining 1 cup flour, 1 teaspoon salt and 1 teaspoon pepper, baking soda and club soda in a small bowl to make the fry batter.

Place a cooling rack over a rimmed baking sheet and set aside. In an electric fryer or a 2-quart saucepan, heat 3 inches cooking oil to 400°.

Remove the goat cheese rounds from the refrigerator and dredge the rounds in the seasoned flour. One by one, dip in the fry batter and carefully place in the hot oil. Without overcrowding the pan, cook the goat cheese until golden brown, turning as needed. When the rounds are golden brown on all sides and floating, remove with a slotted spoon to the prepared rack. Make sure the oil heats back to 400° before adding the second batch. Continue frying until all rounds are done.

To serve, arrange the goat cheese rounds on individual small or tapas size plates. Drizzle with honey and sprinkle with freshly cracked black pepper. Serve immediately.

Garlic Shrimp with Olive Oil and Fresh Bay

{ Serves 6 }

½ cup olive oil
4 cloves garlic, crushed
2 bay leaves
½ teaspoon crushed red pepper flakes
1 pound fresh Georgia shrimp, peeled and deveined
Kosher salt

~

Heat a medium sauté pan over medium heat. Add olive oil and swirl to coat pan. Add garlic, bay leaves and red pepper flakes and sauté until fragrant. Season both sides of shrimp with salt and add to the sauté pan. Sauté 2 minutes, turn shrimp, and cook another 2 minutes, just until shrimp are curled, pink and cooked through. Serve shrimp piping hot in a small crock.

"I sing 'Loving You' in the kitchen all the time. The best part of my job is the interaction with other chefs."

Roasted Baby Beets with Saba

{ Serves 6 }

1 pound baby beets
3 tablespoons olive oil
1 teaspoon kosher salt
½ teaspoon freshly ground pepper
1 ounce saba*
Sea salt and freshly ground pepper
Micro-greens or freshly chopped parsley for garnish

~

Preheat oven to 325°.

Cut the stems from the beets and wash and trim off hairy roots. If beets are large, slice in half or quarters. Place beets on a large piece of aluminum foil, drizzle with oil, season with salt and pepper, and toss to coat. Wrap the beets tightly and place on a rimmed baking sheet. Bake until fork tender, about 40 minutes. Test for doneness. Some beets may take a little longer to become tender.

Remove from the oven, carefully open the foil to release steam and bake, with the foil open, another 12 minutes. Remove skins with a paring knife. Arrange beets on serving platter, sprinkle with salt and pepper and drizzle with saba. Garnish with micro-greens or finely chopped parsley. This is an excellent side dish for beef, lamb and poultry.

*Saba is a slightly sweet, unfermented syrup made from the must of Trebbiano grapes, the same grapes that balsamic vinegar is made from, and is actually a by-product of balsamic vinegar. It is widely used in Italy in sweet and savory cooking.

"I'm obsessed with people being happy. I like to try and get people to relax."

Fig Glazed Rack of Lamb
with Chicory and Warm Potato Salad

{ Serves 4 }

2 lamb racks, bones Frenched
¼ cup Fig Glaze
2 Russet or Idaho potatoes
¼ cup plus 1 tablespoon olive oil, divided
3 ounces goat cheese
2 tablespoons champagne vinegar
1 tablespoon mustard seeds
1 tablespoon fresh tarragon, chiffonade
2 cups fresh chicory or curly endive or radicchio (if using radicchio, cut into 1-inch strips)
Kosher salt and freshly ground pepper

~

Rub lamb racks with ¼ cup of fig glaze, place in a zip-top plastic bag and let marinate overnight in the refrigerator. Scrub the potatoes and cut each potato into 8 thick wedges. Soak in cold water overnight in the refrigerator.

Preheat oven to 400° and preheat the grill to medium.

Drain the soaked potatoes and rub with salt. Place in strainer over a bowl and let the potatoes drain again for 30 minutes. The potatoes should release some liquid in this time. Wash potatoes and pat dry with paper towels, toss with 1 tablespoon oil and spread in a single layer on a rimmed baking sheet. Roast in oven until golden and crisp, about 40 minutes.

While the potatoes are roasting, grill the lamb over medium heat to 140° for rare, about 6 minutes per side. Cooking time will vary greatly depending on the size of the racks, so use a meat thermometer for best results. Remove the lamb from the grill and set aside for 5 minutes to rest. While lamb is resting, toss the warm potatoes with goat cheese, vinegar, mustard seeds, tarragon, remaining ¼ cup olive oil and chicory to make the salad.

Divide the potato salad between 4 warm plates. Cut the lamb into chops and place on the beds of potato salad. Serve the remaining fig glaze on the side.

FIG GLAZE

½ cup fig vinegar
½ cup muscavado, Demerara or turbinado "raw" sugar

~

In a small bowl, whisk the vinegar with the sugar to combine.

Oak Grilled Asparagus with Marinated Tomato Salad

{ Serves 4 }

½ cup oak wood chips
¼ cup plus 2 tablespoons extra virgin olive oil, divided
¼ cup white balsamic vinegar
1 heaping tablespoon finely chopped shallots
1 heaping tablespoon finely chopped parsley
1 heaping tablespoon salt-packed capers; rinsed and finely chopped
½ cup oil-cured olives, pitted and chopped
12 medium cherry tomatoes, cut into eighths
Kosher salt and freshly ground pepper
1 pound white asparagus (green asparagus is fine if no white available)

~

Place the oak chips in a bowl and cover with water. Set aside.

Combine ¼ cup oil, vinegar, shallots, parsley, capers, and olives in a medium bowl. Add the tomatoes and season to taste with salt and pepper. Marinate the salad at room temperature 1 hour before serving.

In a large bowl, mix ice and cold water to make an ice bath; set aside. Bring a large pot of salted water to a boil. Break off the tough ends of the asparagus and discard. Peel away the skin of the bottom 3 inches of the stalks with a vegetable peeler. Drop the asparagus in the boiling water and cook until just tender, 2-3 minutes. Remove and immediately immerse in ice bath to stop the cooking. Transfer the asparagus to a medium bowl and drizzle with the remaining 2 tablespoons of oil; season with salt and pepper.

Heat a grill to medium. Strain oak chips and scatter over the hot coals. Grill the asparagus and cook until blistered, about 3 minutes, turning when beginning to char. Remove to a serving platter and top with the marinated tomato salad.

WHAT TO DRINK

Allow rosé to be your guide on your rendezvous. Thirst quenching and easy going pinks from the South of France set the bar. These wines are as flexible as they are refreshing, since they're bone dry with a floral bouquet and strawberries on the palate.

MICAH WILLIX

wanted to be a cook when he was a kid, then he decided he wanted to become a pilot. It wasn't until high school when he truly decided he wanted to be a cook…again. A filet knife is his essential tool. He buys the same brand and type every time one wears down, but he never throws the old ones away. He has a collection of older knives that he still uses depending on his mood. "My filet knife is the one thing that's the same every day. It's like a blanket."

What's the strangest thing you've ever eaten?
Blood soup in the Philippines. It's basically warmed up cow's blood with bread, similar to bread pudding.

What other jobs have you had?
At one point I was an underwater cement worker. I laid cement on sea walls.

What's your favorite movie?
Any Peter Sellers film.

What food do you find most difficult to work with?
Eggs.

What was the first dish you learned to cook?
Spaghetti with Hunt's tomato sauce.

What would you do if you won the lottery?
I don't play the lotto for fear of winning. It'd destroy my life.

Finish the sentence, I wish I could …
Fly. Because I'd be able to spend time above everything.

Where would you like to visit?
Australia. It seems rugged and diverse. I could spend forever there and never do everything there is to do.

39

MICHAEL TUOHY

WOODFIRE GRILL

Romantic Dinner for Two

—

Marinated Red Ace Beets with Arugula, Goat Cheese
and White Truffle Oil

Roasted Butternut Squash Soup with Grated Pecorino and Saba

Sautéed Porcini Mushrooms with
Anson Mills Polenta, Parmigiano-Reggiano, and Balsamico

Grilled Sonoma Duck Breast with Fingerling Potatoes
and Sun-dried Cherry Jam

Wood Grilled Black Mission Figs
with Greek Yogurt and Wildflower Honey

Marinated Red Ace Beets with Arugula, Goat Cheese and White Truffle Oil

{ Serves 2 }

½ pound Red Ace beets, trimmed of greens and root ends
½ cup cider vinegar
1 cup granulated sugar
1 piece star anise
½ cinnamon stick
1½ teaspoons coriander seeds
2 tablespoons extra virgin olive oil
Kosher salt or sea salt to taste
2 ounces Sweet Grass Dairy fresh goat cheese, crumbled
2 teaspoons white truffle oil

~

Place beets in a 2-quart saucepan and add enough water to cover. Bring to a boil and reduce heat to a low boil and cook beets until fork tender, about 25 minutes.

While beets are cooking, combine cider vinegar, sugar, star anise, cinnamon stick and coriander in a small saucepan. Bring mixture to a boil and stir until sugar is dissolved. Remove from the heat and cool to room temperature. When beets are cool enough to handle, remove skins and discard. Place beets in a glass container. Pour marinade over the beets, cover and refrigerate overnight.

Remove beets from marinade, slice some and cut some in large dice.

Wash arugula and put in a salad spinner. Place arugula in a large bowl, sprinkle with salt and drizzle with olive oil. Toss the arugula leaves to evenly coat with the oil.

Arrange arugula on salad plates. Top with a mixture of sliced and diced beets, sprinkle with goat cheese and drizzle with white truffle oil. Serve immediately.

"I live by seasonality. I once had a pastry chef who wanted to buy blueberries in December. I said no."

Roasted Butternut Squash Soup with Grated Pecorino and Saba

{ Serves 6 }

1 small butternut squash
1 tablespoon grapeseed oil
1 cup roughly chopped onion
1 stalk roughly chopped celery
1½ teaspoons ground cinnamon
1½ teaspoons ground ginger
1½ teaspoons ground coriander
2 cups reduced sodium chicken stock (or vegetable stock)
½ cup apple cider
¼ cup unsalted butter
1 tablespoon honey
1 teaspoon kosher salt
½ teaspoon freshly ground white pepper
1 cup heavy whipping cream (optional)
2 tablespoons saba*
¼ cup finely grated pecorino cheese (or Parmigiano-Reggiano)

Preheat oven to 450°. With a fork or a skewer, prick holes in the butternut squash. Put butternut squash on a baking sheet and place in preheated oven and roast until tender, about 45 minutes. Remove baked butternut squash from oven and allow to cool. When butternut squash is cool enough to handle, split in half, remove and discard seeds and scoop the pulp from the skin. Set pulp aside.

In a 3-quart heavy-bottom pot, heat the grapeseed oil on medium heat. Add onion and celery and cook until soft and translucent, about 5 minutes. Do not allow vegetables to brown. Add reserved butternut squash pulp, cinnamon, ginger, coriander, chicken stock and apple cider. Bring mixture to a boil, then lower heat and simmer the mixture for 45 minutes.

Remove soup from heat and add butter, honey, salt and white pepper. Stir the mixture and add cream. Taste for seasoning and correct seasoning by adding additional salt or pepper.

With an immersion hand blender, purée soup until smooth and creamy. Alternately, soup can be puréed in a blender, working in batches and being careful with the hot liquid.

To serve, ladle 6 ounces of soup into a serving bowl. Sprinkle the pecorino cheese on the top and drizzle the saba decoratively on top. Serve immediately. Leftover soup can be frozen in an airtight container for up to 3 months.

* Saba is a slightly sweet unfermented syrup made from the must of Trebbiano grapes, the same grapes that balsamic vinegar is made from, and is actually a by-product of balsamic vinegar. It is widely used in Italy in sweet and savory cooking. It can be found in specialty food stores.

Sautéed Porcini Mushrooms with Anson Mills Polenta, Parmigiano-Reggiano and Balsamico

{ Serves 2 }

PORCINI
¼ pound porcini mushrooms*
1 tablespoon unsalted butter
2 teaspoons grapeseed oil
2 teaspoons minced garlic
1½ teaspoons finely chopped fresh thyme
1½ teaspoons finely chopped fresh rosemary
¼ cup white wine
½ teaspoon sea salt
¼ teaspoon freshly ground pepper

POLENTA
1½ cups chicken stock, low sodium
½ cup organic polenta, such as Anson Mills
2 tablespoons butter
½ teaspoon kosher salt

GARNISH
2 tablespoons Parmigiano-Reggiano, grated
1 teaspoon aged balsamic vinegar*
1 tablespoon finely chopped parsley

~

For this preparation, the porcini mushrooms need to be cooked before the polenta. The cooked porcini mushrooms can wait, but the polenta will congeal and harden if left in the pan too long. The polenta can be re-warmed, but it is best when served immediately after cooking.

With a mushroom brush, gently remove any dirt and grit from stems of mushrooms. It is important to remove all dirt and grit but to avoid vigorous washing of mushrooms. If necessary, use a wet paper towel to remove stubborn dirt and grit. Trim a sliver off the stem of each mushroom and slice lengthwise leaving stem intact where possible.

In a 10-inch cast iron skillet or other heavy sauté pan, heat grapeseed oil and butter on medium heat. When butter has melted, add the porcini mushrooms and toss to coat. Sauté the mushrooms until they begin to brown and caramelize, about 4 minutes. Add garlic, thyme and rosemary and continue to cook for 2-3 more minutes. When mushrooms are nicely brown and caramelized, add white wine to deglaze pan. Let all liquid evaporate. Season with salt and pepper and set aside.

In a 2-quart saucepan, bring chicken stock to a boil. Lower heat so that chicken stock is at a simmer, and add polenta in a steady stream while whisking mixture. Reduce heat to low and cook polenta until it is thick and creamy, about 8-10 minutes. Add butter and salt. The grains should be thick and creamy. If the polenta does not seem creamy and thick, add a little more chicken stock and whisk mixture until all liquid is absorbed.

Place a scoop of polenta on each plate. Place half the cooked porcini on top of polenta. Grate the Parmigiano-Reggiano directly on top of the porcini, drizzle with balsamic vinegar and garnish with chopped parsley.

* Porcini mushrooms can be found in specialty grocery stores. Other exotic mushrooms can be used as well.
* Balsamic vinegar can be boiled down to a syrupy stage if your budget will not allow an aged one.

"I almost became a San Francisco fireman instead of a chef."

Grilled Sonoma Duck Breast with Fingerling Potatoes and Sun-dried Cherry Jam

{ Serves 2 }

1 whole Magret duck breast*
Kosher salt and freshly ground white pepper
1 cup sun-dried cherries
⅓ cup granulated sugar
1¼ cups water
1 tablespoon freshly squeezed lemon juice
2 tablespoons balsamic vinegar

¼ cup ruby port wine
½ pound fingerling potatoes
¾ cup rendered duck fat
¼ cup finely chopped rosemary
Fleur de sel for garnish
Chives for garnish

~

Trim the duck breast of excess fat, leaving a thin layer intact. Add the trimmed fat to the rendered fat for future use. Using a paring knife, score the skin side of the duck breast, cutting through the skin and fat only, not into the flesh. Cut on a diagonal across the breast, leaving ½-inch between each score. Repeat in opposite direction to form a diamond pattern. Season both sides of breast with salt and white pepper. Allow to sit at room temperature for 30 minutes before grilling. You can season several hours ahead of time and refrigerate until needed.

In a heavy-bottom 2-quart saucepan, combine the cherries, sugar, water, lemon juice, vinegar and port. Bring to a low boil, reduce heat to low, and simmer for 45 minutes. Cool to room temperature. Process with an immersion blender until the mixture is thick and resembles jam. Set aside until ready to serve.

Slice any large fingerling potatoes in half lengthwise. Keep smaller ones whole. Place potatoes in a large saucepan and cover with water, add 1 tablespoon salt, turn on high heat and bring to a boil. Reduce heat to a gentle simmer and cook just until fork tender, about 13 minutes, being careful not to overcook. Drain in a colander and spread on a towel lined sheet pan to dry.

Heat grill and allow wood or charcoal to develop white hot coals before placing duck on grill. Place the breasts skin side down on the grill. Do not place the breasts directly over the flames. Grill for about 10 minutes and, as fat renders, rotate for even cooking. Turn and continue cooking to desired doneness, about 8 more minutes for rare. Food safety guidelines recommend cooking to a minimal internal temperature of 160°. I recommend cooking duck breast rare to medium-rare.

While the duck is cooking, heat a medium, heavy-bottom sauté pan over medium-high heat. Add duck fat. The fat should be about ¼-inch deep. Add the now dry potatoes, rosemary and a little kosher salt and gently toss to coat the potatoes. Heat through, about 5 minutes. Remove the potatoes to a paper towel lined plate to drain and serve immediately.

The potatoes should be ready at the same time the duck is finished. Allow the duck breast to rest for 1 minute after removing from the grill. Slice duck breast into ½-inch slices on the bias, then fan on the plate. Place the hot potatoes onto the plate along with the duck breast. Add a spoonful of cherry jam, a quenelle shape, to the plate. Sprinkle fleur de sel and chives on the duck.

* Magret duck is available at Sonoma Saveurs. Visit www.sonomasaveurs.com or Woodfire Café.

Wood Grilled Black Mission Figs with Greek Yogurt and Wildflower Honey

{ Serves 2 }

½ pint plain Greek yogurt
¼ cup balsamic vinegar
¼ cup grapeseed oil
1 teaspoon freshly ground pepper
2 teaspoons lemon zest
½ pint black Mission figs, stemmed and halved
1 tablespoon wildflower honey
1 tablespoon finely chopped fresh mint

~

Drain yogurt in a fine mesh sieve placed over a bowl to remove any excess moisture.

In a medium bowl, whisk the vinegar, oil, pepper and lemon zest to combine. Add the prepared figs and gently toss to coat. Cover and marinate for 1-2 hours.

Heat a grill to medium. Place the marinated figs on the grill, cut-side down, for 2 minutes, turn and continue grilling for 1 minute and remove.

Divide the yogurt equally between 2 serving bowls. Divide the figs between the bowls and drizzle a little wildflower honey onto each. Garnish with mint and serve.

WHAT TO DRINK

Spanish is a language of love. Spanish red wine is one of romance. The native Iberian varietal, tempranillo, is the grape that makes folks recall their Spanish vacation with a faraway look in their eyes. This delicate gem produces wines balanced and food friendly with an enviable swagger from years of experience in the realm of amor. Spain's most famous region for the red is Rioja with Ribera del Duero moving into a close second spot of fame. Be sure to allow the wine to breathe before serving.

MICHAEL TUOHY

comments, "I wish I could make everyone eat great food." He was an early advocate of using local
organic farmed produce. He delights in offering seasonal products from small local farms,
fire-roasting and grilling them for his guests at Woodfire Grill.
"Growing up we had lots of fresh vegetables. Dinners
would be steak and Dungeness crab."

What's your most used quote in the kitchen?
"Taste." "Keep it fresh."
"Where did it come from?"

If you could have a different occupation for one day, what would it be?
A real estate developer
or farmer.

If you could have a theme song playing every time you walk into the kitchen, what would it be?
"Let Me Stand Next to
Your Fire" by Jimi Hendrix.

Do you have words to live by?
Keep it fresh. Keep it simple.
Look for better ways.

Where were you born?
San Francisco. I came to
Atlanta to open Chefs' Café.

Where would you like to visit?
I would love to visit Australia.
They have tremendous food
sensibilities in Australia.

What would you do if you won the lottery?
I'd make sure everything I owe is
paid off. Then I'd put the money
into interest bearing securities. I'd
identify some organizations to help,
probably in food distribution. And
I'd definitely take a few trips!

ELISA GAMBINO

Dinner with the Gambinos

Bruschetta with Pomodorini

Straccetti e Rucola

Leek and Ricotta Cannelloni with Basil Oil

Spinach and Ricotta Gnocchi with Brown Butter and Pine Nuts

Sgroppino

Bruschetta with Pomodorini

BRUSCHETTA WITH CHERRY TOMATOES

{ Serves 6 }

1 pint of cherry tomatoes, cut into eighths
2 cloves fresh garlic
1 bunch fresh basil
Kosher salt and freshly ground pepper
1 loaf of good, slightly stale, dense, rustic Italian-style bread
4 tablespoons extra virgin olive oil, divided

~

Combine the tomatoes and 1 clove of sliced garlic in a medium bowl. Remove thick stems from basil and tear most of the bunch into small pieces (reserve remaining leaves for garnish). Add the torn basil leaves to the tomato mixture and stir in 3 tablespoons extra virgin olive oil; season with kosher salt and pepper to taste. Stir and let rest for 1 hour.

Meanwhile, slice the bread, on an angle, ½-inch thick. Set the oven rack 6 inches from the broiler and preheat to low. Place sliced bread on a rimmed baking sheet and place under the broiler for 2-3 minutes until golden brown on one side. Remove, turn the bread over and toast lightly on the other side. (Watch the bread carefully because it will toast quickly.) Cut the remaining garlic clove in half. After the bread is toasted on both sides remove from the oven and brush one side with the remaining tablespoon of extra virgin olive oil and season lightly with kosher salt. Place the bread back under the broiler to heat the oil, about 15 seconds. Remove the bread from the oven and rub with the cut side of the garlic. Place the toasts on a platter and spoon a little of the tomato mixture on top of each piece. Garnish with basil leaves and serve immediately.

"I really became interested in cooking when I was a teenager living in Italy. Both my parents loved to entertain and we always had company. I helped plan the menu, shop at the market and prepare the meal."

Straccetti e Rucola

BEEF STRIPS WITH ARUGULA

{ Serves 4 to 6 }

1 pound beef tenderloin
2 cloves finely chopped garlic
¼ cup extra virgin olive oil
½ teaspoon dried rosemary
½ teaspoon dried sage
Sea salt and freshly ground pepper
8 ounces baby arugula, washed and dried
1 lemon

~

Place the tenderloin in the freezer and chill until firm, at least 30 minutes. In a small bowl, whisk to combine the garlic, olive oil, rosemary and sage. Season to taste with salt and pepper.

Divide the arugula between 4 chilled plates. Cover with a damp paper towel until ready to serve.

Remove the tenderloin from the freezer and slice on the diagonal as thinly as possible. Toss the thinly sliced tenderloin in the dressing until well coated. Heat a large heavy-bottom skillet on medium-high until hot, but not smoking. With a fork, remove the tenderloin from the dressing and place in the hot pan. Cook, turning after 1 minute. Remove the cooked tenderloin from the skillet and add directly to the baby arugula. Add remainder of the marinade to the pan and bring to a boil. Drizzle the hot marinade over the salads, squeeze lemon over the top and season with sea salt to taste. Serve immediately.

Leek and Ricotta Cannelloni with Basil Oil

{ Serves 6 to 8 }

2 leeks
2 cups fresh sheep's milk ricotta
1 tablespoon extra virgin olive oil, additional for baking dish
¼ cup freshly grated Parmigiano-Reggiano
1 large egg, lightly beaten
20 5- x 5-inch fresh pasta squares*
Kosher salt to taste
Tomato Sauce
Basil Oil

~

Cut the white part from the leeks and rinse well, removing all mud, grit and dirt. Slice the leeks into very thin rounds. Heat a 10-inch sauté pan over medium heat, add oil and swirl to cover the bottom of the pan. Add leeks and sauté until they are translucent and beginning to caramelize, about 10 minutes.

Place a cooling rack on a rimmed baking sheet and set aside. Fill a large soup pot with water, add 1 tablespoon salt and bring to a boil. Add the fresh pasta sheets and cook al denté, according to package directions. Carefully remove the sheets from the water and lay flat on the prepared rack to drain. Pat dry with paper towels.

Remove the leeks from the pan, cool slightly, and finely chop. In large mixing bowl, combine the ricotta, Parmigiano-Reggiano and the egg, stir to mix well. Fold the leeks into the ricotta mixture and season with salt to taste. Spoon the mixture into a pastry bag, twist to secure the end and pipe the filling lengthwise along the bottom edge of the cooked pasta. Tightly roll the pasta into a tube and slice into three equal pieces. Repeat with remaining pasta squares and filling.

Preheat the oven to 350°. Lightly brush an 11- x 7-inch baking dish with oil. Spread a ladle of tomato sauce in the dish to cover the bottom. Cut the filled cannelloni noodles in thirds. Stand the cannelloni in the dish, cut sides up, filling the dish. It is fine if the cannelloni are crowded. Cover the dish with aluminum foil and bake for 30 minutes. Remove from the oven and cool and set for 10 minutes prior to serving.

To serve, spread a ladle of tomato sauce on each warm dinner plate, place 2 cannelloni, cut side up onto the sauce and drizzle with basil oil. Serve immediately.

If you need to, best quality dry cannelloni noodles may be substituted. Cook according to package instructions.

* Fresh pasta can be purchased from Via Elisa Fresh Pasta. Call for availability or to place an order 404-605-0668.

TOMATO SAUCE

¼ cup extra virgin olive oil
2 cloves finely chopped fresh garlic
1 finely chopped carrot
1 finely chopped celery stalk
1 28-ounce can peeled, whole San Marzano tomatoes
5 fresh basil leaves, chiffonade
Kosher salt and freshly ground pepper to taste

~

Heat a large saucepan over medium-high heat. Add olive oil and swirl the pan to coat the bottom. Add the garlic, carrot and celery and cook until fragrant, about 2 minutes. Add tomatoes and juice and cook over moderately high heat, until sauce thickens, about 30 minutes. Using an immersion blender, pulse the sauce until it is coarsely ground. Stir in the basil leaves and season with salt and pepper to taste.

BASIL OIL

1 large bunch of fresh basil
1 cup extra virgin olive oil

~

Rinse the basil and remove any large, tough stems. Fill a large mixing bowl with ice and water to create an ice bath; set aside. Bring a 2-quart saucepan of water to a boil. In small batches, drop the basil leaves into the boiling water for 15 seconds. Remove the basil with a slotted spoon and drop into the ice bath for 30 seconds to stop the cooking. Repeat until finished. Place the blanched basil leaves onto paper towels. Roll tightly and squeeze until there is no water remaining. Chop the basil and place into a glass jar. Pour 1 cup of extra virgin olive oil over the basil and let it sit for 4 hours or overnight. Strain the oil through a cheese cloth, squeezing to remove all oil. Discard the blanched basil and reserve the oil.

Spinach and Ricotta Gnocchi with Brown Butter and Pine Nuts

{ Serves 6 to 8 }

6 ounces finely chopped cooked spinach, squeezed dry
10 ounces fresh sheep's milk ricotta
Kosher salt
Freshly ground nutmeg
1 large egg, lightly beaten
¼ cup freshly grated aged Parmigiano-Reggiano
3 tablespoons all-purpose flour, additional for dusting
Brown Butter Sauce
¼ cup toasted pine nuts

~

Combine the spinach, ricotta, and a pinch each of salt and nutmeg in a medium saucepan and cook, gently stirring, for 5 minutes over medium heat. Remove from the heat and stir in the egg, Parmigiano-Reggiano and the flour. Mix well. Transfer the mixture to a metal or glass bowl, cover and chill the mixture for at least 4 hours. Once chilled and set, remove ½ cup of the ricotta mixture onto a floured surface and gently shape into a small cylinder, about 1 inch in diameter. Cut the cylinder into smaller cylinders, 1 inch long, and lightly dust in flour, gently tossing to remove any excess.

Bring a large pot of salted water to a boil. Place the gnocchi into the boiling water, reduce the heat to a low boil and poach. Once the gnocchi are floating, remove with a slotted spoon and place in a large, flat pasta bowl. Gently toss with the brown butter sauce, garnish with toasted pine nuts and serve immediately.

BROWN BUTTER SAUCE

5 tablespoons unsalted butter, divided
¼ cup dry white wine
2 tablespoons finely chopped shallots
1 teaspoon finely chopped garlic
2 teaspoons freshly squeezed lemon juice, or to taste
Salt and freshly ground pepper

~

In a small heavy-bottom saucepan, heat 3 tablespoons butter over medium heat until browned with a slight nutty aroma. Add the wine, shallots and garlic. Simmer until reduced to about 3 tablespoons. Cut the remaining 2 tablespoons butter into small cubes. When the butter sauce has reduced, lower the heat and whisk in the cubed butter just until combined. Do not overheat. Remove pan from heat and stir in lemon juice and season with salt and pepper to taste.

As a field producer based in Rome and Moscow for CNN, Gambino was never far from fresh Italian food. "I always traveled with a full supply of Italian foods and whenever possible, I cooked pasta in my hotel room on a small hotplate."

Sgroppino

{ Serves 4 }

2 cups of lemon gelato (lemon sorbet may be substituted)
½ cup chilled vodka
¼ cup heavy whipping cream
1 cup chilled Prosecco

Place the sorbet, vodka and whipping cream in the container of a blender. Blend on high until smooth. Add Prosecco and blend just until combined. Pour into chilled fluted glasses and serve immediately.

WHAT TO DRINK

With these Italian classics, stick with Italian classic wines. Hailing from Italy's renowned red wine region, Piedmont, Gavi di Gavi serves as western Italy's fruity and aromatic white wine ambassador. Allow the wine to tarry until the tenderloin makes its appearance.

The spicy bacon flavor of the arugula melding with the tender beef should be pure ecstasy when matched with Italy's most famous red, Chianti. Immediately fruity with earthy balance, the wine can take you through the gnocchi and into late dinner conversations.

ELISA GAMBINO

credits her mother with having the most inspiration on her career. "My mother was an amazing cook who made it her mission to bring us together every evening for a delicious meal." While it is clear that Elisa Gambino is a natural in the kitchen, she certainly didn't start out knowing she wanted to own her own pasta company. "As a kid I wanted to be a social worker and peace activist." Gambino ended up spending 15 years traveling the globe as a producer for CNN before turning to the kitchen.

What's your favorite guilty pleasure?
Eating Phatty Cake cookies.

What's your fondest childhood memory?
Finding a blue velvet winter coat under the Christmas tree when I was 10.

What's an accomplishment you're most proud of?
I'm most proud of convincing my husband to marry me.

What's your most memorable moment?
Meeting Nelson Mandela during the first free elections in South Africa.

If you could have a theme song playing every time you walk into the kitchen, what would it be?
"Bring It On" by Seal because Seal is so sexy and I'd like to have him in my kitchen.

If you were on a deserted island and could only take one kitchen tool what would it be?
I'd take my food mill so my sauce would be nice and smooth.

Who's the most famous person you've cooked for?
Paul McCartney and his band.

What's your favorite book?
An American Tragedy by Theodore Dreiser.

GERRY KLASKALA

{ ARIA }

Dinner for Your Foodie Friends

—

Lobster Minestrone with Swiss Chard, Leeks and Borlotti Beans

Sweet and Spicy Prawns with Pear and Cashew Salad

Fresh Pappardelle with Rabbit and Porcini Ragout

Copper River King Salmon with Spring Peas, Vidalia Onion
and Applewood Smoked Bacon

Orange Chocolate Mousse Cake

Lobster Minestrone with Swiss Chard, Leeks and Borlotti Beans

{ Serves 6 }

½ cup dried borlotti beans (cranberry or pinto beans may be substituted)
3 lobster tails
2 tablespoons olive oil, more for brushing lobsters
Kosher salt and freshly ground pepper
½ cup ½-inch diced onion
2 leeks, rinsed well, white parts cut into a ½-inch dice
½ cup ¼-inch diced celery
¼ cup ¼-inch diced carrots
2 teaspoons finely minced garlic
2 cups rough chopped tomato
4 sprigs fresh thyme
1 sprig fresh tarragon
½ cup dry white wine
4 cups light chicken or seafood stock
1 bunch Swiss chard, tough stems discarded
½ cup roughly chopped Italian parsley
1 cup cooked bow tie pasta

~

Soak the beans overnight in a large heavy-bottom Dutch oven in 3 cups of water. Drain and rinse. Place drained beans back in pot and add enough water to come 2 inches over the beans. Cook until tender, about 3 hours.

With a very large chef knife, cut lobster tails in half lengthwise. Brush the cut side of the lobster with olive oil and season with salt and pepper. Heat a heavy-bottom 4-quart saucepan over medium-high heat. Add the 2 tablespoons olive oil and swirl to cover bottom of the pan. Place lobsters shell side down and cook until the meat begins to set, about 4 minutes. The lobster tails will curl and the meat will start turning opaque. Turn lobsters over and cook for 30 seconds. Remove the pan from the heat and remove the lobsters. Remove the meat from the shells and return the lobster shells to the pan. Dice the lobster meat and set aside.

Return the pan with the lobster shells to the stove and heat over medium-high heat. Add the onion and leeks and cook for 5 minutes. Add celery, carrots and garlic and cook another 5 minutes, stirring occasionally. Add tomatoes, thyme and tarragon and cook another 3 minutes. Add white wine and cook until reduced and almost completely dry. Add the stock and bring to a boil. Reduce heat and simmer 45 minutes. Remove the lobster shells. Cut the Swiss chard into shreds and add to the soup and cook another 10 minutes. Add the cooked beans and parsley. Season to taste with salt and pepper.

To serve, divide the pasta between 6 warmed soup bowls, add the lobster and ladle in the hot minestrone and serve.

Sweet and Spicy Prawns with Pear and Cashew Salad

{ Serves 4 }

1 pound jumbo prawns (8 to the pound), peeled and deveined
1 tablespoon canola oil, additional for cooking
1 tablespoon finely minced fresh ginger
1 tablespoon plus 1 teaspoon finely minced fresh cilantro, additional for garnish
1 teaspoon finely minced fresh garlic
¼ cup Mae Ploy sweet chili sauce
1 teaspoon finely minced fresh chives
2 teaspoons freshly squeezed lime juice
Pear and Cashew Salad
3 scallions, rinsed, trimmed and sliced on the diagonal for garnish

~

Combine prawns with canola oil, ginger, 1 tablespoon cilantro and garlic. Cover and marinate in refrigerator for 2 hours.

For the sweet and spicy sauce, combine the chili sauce, chives, remaining 1 teaspoon cilantro and lime juice in a small bowl. Mix to combine and set aside. While the prawns are marinating, make the pear salad.

To serve, heat a large sauté pan over medium-high heat and add just enough canola oil to coat the bottom of the pan. Add the marinated prawns and sauté until curled and pink, about 3 minutes. Turn and continue cooking until opaque, about 2 more minutes. Place a small mound of the salad on the plate, top with the cooked prawns and decoratively drizzle the plate with the sweet and spicy sauce. Garnish with cilantro sprigs and scallions.

PEAR AND CASHEW SALAD

¼ cup Mae Ploy sweet chili sauce
1 medium shallot, peeled
1 clove garlic, peeled
1 small Thai red chili
2 tablespoons freshly squeezed lime juice
½ teaspoon kosher salt
¼ cup canola oil

1 pear, peeled, cored and cut into 2-inch matchsticks
1 cup white cabbage, cut into 2-inch matchsticks
¼ cup coarsely chopped cilantro leaves
1 tablespoon salted, roasted cashews, crushed

~

In a blender combine the chili sauce, shallot, garlic, chili, lime juice, and kosher salt. Blend to combine. With the blender running, in a slow, steady stream, drizzle in the canola oil. In a large bowl, combine the drained pear, cabbage, cilantro and cashews and toss with tongs. Add just enough dressing (about 2-3 tablespoons) to lightly coat and toss to combine.

Fresh Pappardelle with Rabbit and Porcini Ragout

{ Serves 4 }

1 whole French rabbit
3 tablespoons olive oil, divided
1 cup ¾-inch diced onion
1 cup ½-inch diced celery
¼ cup ½-inch diced carrots
1 leek, halved, rinsed well and diced
2 whole garlic cloves, peeled
2 bay leaves
12 shiitake mushrooms, wiped clean, stems removed and reserved
1 cup dried porcini mushrooms
1 cup ¼-inch diced onion
1 celery root, peeled and cut into ¼-inch dice
¼ cup ¼-inch diced carrot
2 tablespoons tomato paste
1 tablespoon finely minced garlic
1 cup dry white wine
Kosher salt and freshly ground pepper
1 tablespoon unsalted butter
½ cup chopped Italian parsley
½ cup grated Parmigiano-Reggiano
1 pound fresh pappardelle pasta

~

Debone the rabbit, reserving the meat and bones. Dice the rabbit meat and set aside. Heat a 4-quart heavy-bottom saucepan over medium-high heat. Add 1 tablespoon olive oil and swirl to cover bottom of pan. Add rabbit bones and sear until lightly browned, about 5 minutes. Add ¾-inch diced onion, ½-inch diced celery, ½-inch diced carrots, leek, garlic cloves, bay leaves and shiitake stems. Add enough water to cover 1 inch over the bones. Bring to a boil, reduce heat and simmer for 2½ hours to make the rabbit stock. Strain and set aside.

Still passionate about art, you can find Gerry on weekends in his garage, painting.

Bring 1 cup water to a boil in a small saucepan. Remove from the heat and add dried porcini mushrooms. Set aside to soak for 1 hour. Strain the soaking liquid through a very fine mesh strainer and reserve. Mince the reconstituted porcini for later use.

Heat a 2½-quart heavy-bottom saucepan over medium-high heat, add 1 tablespoon olive oil and swirl to cover bottom of pan. Lightly season diced rabbit with salt. Add the rabbit to the pan and cook until lightly colored, about 3 minutes. Remove rabbit to a shallow plate and set aside. Return the pot to the heat and add the remaining 1 tablespoon olive oil; swirl to cover the bottom of the pan. Add the ¼-inch diced onions, celery root, ¼-inch diced carrots, shiitake mushroom caps, tomato paste and minced garlic and cook until softened, about 10 minutes. Deglaze with white wine and evaporate, this will only take a minute or so. Add rabbit, minced porcini and reserved porcini soaking liquid. Add enough rabbit stock to cover all and slowly simmer for 1-1½ hours or until the rabbit is tender. Adjust seasoning with salt and pepper.

Fill a large pot with water. Bring to a boil and add 1 teaspoon salt. Add pasta and cook al denté, for fresh pasta, about 3 minutes. Drain pasta in a large colander.

In a large stainless steel bowl, ladle in half the rabbit ragout, add the butter, parsley, and Parmigiano-Reggiano and toss. Add freshly cooked pappardelle and gently toss to combine. Serve in warmed pasta bowls and garnish with fresh curls of Parmigiano-Reggiano.

Copper River King Salmon with Spring Peas, Vidalia Onion and Applewood Smoked Bacon

{ Serves 4 }

2 applewood smoked bacon strips, julienne
2 teaspoons unsalted butter, divided
2 Vidalia spring onions, white part only
1 cup heavy cream
Kosher salt and freshly ground pepper
4 5- to 6-ounce skin on Copper River king salmon filets
3 teaspoons extra virgin olive oil, divided
½ cup spring peas, blanched
1 cup snow pea shoots
1 lemon
Pea Puree

~

Heat a heavy-bottom sauté pan over medium heat, add bacon and cook over medium heat just until it is starting to brown. Remove to a paper towel lined plate and set aside. Reserve pan for cooking fish.

Heat a heavy-bottom 2-quart saucepan over medium heat. Add 1 teaspoon butter and swirl pan to melt. Add onions and slowly cook for 4-6 minutes; if onions begin to brown, reduce the heat. Add cream, increase the heat to medium-high and continue to heat, stirring occasionally when mixture begins to boil up, until cream has thickened to a sauce consistency, about 15 minutes. Remove from heat, taste and season with salt and pepper as needed. Cover to keep warm until ready to serve.

Season salmon filets on both sides with salt. Heat a heavy-bottom sauté pan over medium-high heat. Add 1 teaspoon oil and remaining 1 teaspoon butter. When butter begins to brown, add salmon filets, flesh side down. Cook filets until they have a golden brown crust, about 4 minutes. Turn filets over and cook another 2 minutes. If the filets are over 1-inch thick, cook on the sides as well, turning when the sides are nicely crusted.

To serve, bring the cream sauce to a boil and reduce to a simmer. Add peas and bacon. Season to taste with salt. In a small bowl, toss pea shoots with remaining 2 teaspoons olive oil, 1 teaspoon lemon juice and a pinch of salt.

Spoon 2 tablespoons pea puree onto center of a warm plate, top with a ladle of creamed peas and then with a salmon filet. Garnish with the pea shoot salad and serve immediately.

PEA PUREE

½ cup spring peas, blanched
3 tablespoons chicken or vegetable stock
2 teaspoons unsalted butter
Kosher salt

~

Combine peas, stock, and butter. Bring to a boil and remove from the heat. Place pea mixture in a blender and blend on high. Season to taste with salt. Keep warm.

Orange Chocolate Mousse Cake

{ Serves 8 to 10 }

½ pound semisweet Valrhona chocolate, chopped
2 tablespoons finely minced candied orange peel, additional strips for garnish
4 cups heavy cream
1 tablespoon Grand Marnier
Cocoa powder for garnish

~

Line an 8-inch springform pan with plastic wrap. Set aside.

Fill a saucepan with 3 inches of water and bring to a simmer. Place the chopped chocolate in a large bowl and place over the simmering water. Stir occasionally until the chocolate is melted and smooth. Remove from the heat and stir in candied orange peel. Set aside.

In the bowl of an electric mixer fitted with the whisk attachment, whip the cream and Grand Marnier to soft peaks. Gently fold a little of the whipped cream into the chocolate mixture to lighten and then fold the remaining cream into the chocolate until combined. Spoon the chocolate mixture into the prepared pan and gently press additional plastic wrap on top of the chocolate mixture to cover. Refrigerate overnight to chill and harden.

To serve, remove the plastic wrap from the top. Release the spring to open the pan and gently remove the collar. Peel the plastic wrap from the sides and cut the mousse into wedges. Dust with cocoa powder and garnish each slice with candied orange peel. Serve immediately.

WHAT TO DRINK

Australia's Clare Valley is a varied, picturesque landscape of inimitable beauty. It is here that one of the world's most interesting wines is produced. Bone dry Rieslings in an unmistakably Alsatian style with new world flair, these whites are food wines. Start the meal out with one of these jewels paired with the prawn and cashew salad continuing through the lobster minestrone. Transition into an earthy Oregon Pinot Noir. The rabbit and porcini woodsy flavors will make your tastebuds sing, while the salmon will spell out pure ecstasy.

entered a gourmet food show as an apprentice at age 17. He subsequently took home "best of show" honors, the first time a cooking novice had earned such a prestigious award. He abandoned his professional aspirations in the art world for another passion—culinary artistry—and graduated with honors from the Culinary Institute of America.

What's your favorite vacation spot?
St. John in the Virgin Islands.

What's your favorite place to eat when you're not at your own restaurant?
There's no place like home.

What were your meals at home like growing up?
Meat and potatoes, meat and potatoes, meat and potatoes, etc.

What's your favorite time of day and why?
Twilight, it's just magical.

What did you want to be when you grew up?
An artist.

Where would you like to visit that you've never been before?
Sicily.

If you could have a theme song playing every time you walk into the kitchen, what would it be?
"Rebel Yell" by Billy Idol.

What's your favorite kitchen tool?
My Forschner chef knife.

What's your favorite TV show?
Iron Chef.

What's your all-time favorite movie?
Ang Lee's *Eat Drink Man Woman*.

What would you do if you won the lottery?
I would build the most beautiful restaurant in the world.

SHERI DAVIS

DISH

Cocktail Party

—

Smoked Salmon Pizza

Rosemary Popcorn

Crispy Duck Tacos with Tomatillo Salsa

Mini Crispy Crab Cakes With Mango Coulis

Shrimp Lollipops

Smoked Salmon Pizza

{ Serves 4 }

Pizza Dough
1 finely minced shallot
1 tablespoon freshly squeezed lemon juice
¼ teaspoon granulated sugar
1 tablespoon canola oil
2 tablespoons extra virgin olive oil, additional for brushing
Kosher salt and freshly ground pepper
6 ounces brie cheese, sliced thin
2 cups baby arugula
½ cup seeded and finely diced tomato
1 small, finely diced apple
2 tablespoons finely chopped chives
4 ounces smoked salmon, sliced very thin

~

Preheat the grill to medium-high. Alternately, preheat oven to 450°. If you have a pizza stone, place on lower rack in oven and heat with the oven.

In a small bowl, whisk together the shallot, lemon juice, sugar, canola oil, 2 tablespoons olive oil and a pinch of salt and pepper. Taste with an arugula leaf and adjust seasoning as needed to balance the flavors. Set aside.

Press each dough ball into a round disk. Lightly dust your work surface with flour or corn meal. With a rolling pin, roll each disk into a thin circle, about 6 inches in diameter. Repeat with remaining dough. Lightly brush the top of each crust with olive oil, sprinkle with salt and pepper. Place on the grill and cook, just until starting to set, about 2 minutes. Alternately, slide crust directly onto the heated pizza stone and bake 3 minutes, or just until starting to set. Remove the par baked crust from the grill or oven.

Divide the brie evenly among the pizzas. Place the crust in the oven and cook just until the cheese is melted and the crust is crispy, about 4-6 minutes.

While the pizzas are cooking, toss the arugula, tomato, apple and chives with just enough of the shallot vinaigrette to lightly coat. Remove the pizzas from the oven and cut each pizza into 4 pieces. Place a little arugula salad on each slice of pizza and top with smoked salmon.

"I do a little skateboarding. My kids are trying to get me a long board."

PIZZA DOUGH

{ Makes 3 small pizza crusts }

⅓ cup warm water (110°)
1 tablespoon yeast
1 large egg, lightly beaten
1¾ cups all-purpose flour (use a hard wheat or high gluten flour)
½ teaspoon kosher salt
1 teaspoon extra virgin olive oil

~

Pour the warm water into a small bowl and add the yeast. Using a wire whisk, stir the mixture until the yeast has dissolved and the water has turned a putty color. Let the yeast stand until it becomes foamy, about 5 minutes.

In the bowl of a stand mixer fitted with the paddle attachment, combine the flour, yeast mixture, egg and olive oil. Mix on low until the dough comes together. Sprinkle in salt. The dough should be smooth and soft, not tacky. Pinch the dough between two fingers to test for tackiness. If needed, add flour, a little at a time. Turn the dough out onto a lightly floured surface and knead 4 or 5 times to shape into a ball.

Brush the inside of a medium bowl with olive oil, and place the dough in the bowl. Cover with oiled plastic wrap and place in a warm spot until doubled in size, about 40 minutes.

Punch down the dough and turn out onto a lightly floured surface. Knead 4-5 times by folding the dough over itself. Turn the dough over, folded side down, cover with plastic wrap and return to the warm spot to rise until it has doubled in size again, about 30 minutes.

Punch down the dough again and place on a lightly floured surface. Divide the dough into 3 pieces. Knead each piece 4 or 5 times.

This dough can be made up to 12 hours in advance and refrigerated or frozen for up to 3 months.

Rosemary Popcorn

{ Serves 4 to 6 }

¼ cup 75%-25% olive and canola oil blend
4 large sprigs fresh rosemary
½ cup popcorn kernels
Fine sea salt

~

Warm the oil in a 4-quart saucepan on low heat. Add 3 rosemary sprigs, remove from the heat, set aside and steep the rosemary oil for 2 hours. Remove the rosemary sprigs and heat the oil over high heat, until hot but not smoking. Add popcorn, cover and reduce heat to medium. When the corn starts popping, shake the pan and keep the kernels moving. When popping slows down, continue to shake, remove from the heat, uncover and let rest until the popping stops. Sprinkle with sea salt and pour into a large bowl, layering in a little sea salt as you pour. Toss and season again. Place in smaller bowls and garnish with remaining rosemary. Serve immediately and enjoy the fun! May use different oils or seasonings for the popcorn such as parmesan cheese, crushed red pepper or granulated garlic.

Crispy Duck Tacos with Tomatillo Salsa

{ Serves 6 }

6 duck confit leg quarters (can be found at Whole Foods Market)
½ cup Mae Ploy sweet chili sauce (found at Asian markets)
2 tablespoons sweet soy sauce (found at Asian markets)
3 kaffir lime leaves, very thinly sliced
Kosher salt and freshly ground pepper
12 fresh yellow corn tortillas
1 small package queso fresco (soft, white Mexican cheese), crumbled or grated
1 pound tomatillos
½ cup diced yellow onion
4 cloves garlic
3 fresh jalapeño peppers, stems removed, cored and seeded
2 teaspoons kosher salt
1 bunch fresh cilantro, rinsed well
1 avocado, peeled and pitted
¼ cup freshly squeezed lime juice
Canola oil for frying

~

Heat the duck confit in the microwave or wrapped in foil in a 350° oven until warm. In a small saucepan, mix the chili garlic sauce, sweet soy sauce and lime leaves. Bring mixture to a boil and remove from the heat. Remove the duck meat from the bones and shred. Mix the shredded duck meat with the chili sauce mixture. Set aside.

Place the tortillas in a damp towel and heat in the microwave, a minute or so, until they are pliable. Place a large spoonful of the duck mixture in each tortilla along with a generous sprinkling of queso fresco. Roll the tortillas tightly and secure with a toothpick. Cover with a damp paper towel and refrigerate.

Remove the papery skin from the tomatillos, rinse in hot water and rub to remove dirt and sticky residue. Quarter the tomatillos. In a large saucepan, combine tomatillos, onion, garlic, jalapeño and 2 teaspoons salt. Add just enough water to cover. Bring to a boil and reduce heat to a simmer. Simmer until the tomatillos are soft. Drain and cool. Place the tomatillo mixture and ¼ cup water in a blender and purée until smooth. Add the cilantro, avocado and lime juice and blend until smooth. Taste and adjust seasoning with salt as needed to balance the bitter and sour flavors. Chill the salsa until ready to serve.

Place a cooling rack over a rimmed baking sheet; set aside. Heat a cast iron Dutch oven over medium-high heat. Add 4 inches canola oil and heat to 350°. Fry the tightly rolled duck tacos a few at a time, without crowding the pan, until golden and crispy, about 4 minutes. Drain on the prepared rack. Cut the taco at an angle and stand the two pieces on a plate. Serve with the tomatillo salsa. (This is also great as duck nachos. Serve the shredded duck on a crispy tortilla chip. Top with queso fresco and a dollop of tomatillo salsa.)

Mini Crispy Crab Cakes with Mango Coulis

{ Serves 8 }

3 ripe mangos
⅓ cup freshly squeezed lime juice
Kosher salt and freshly ground white pepper
1 pound jumbo lump crab meat
3 tablespoons finely diced red bell pepper
½ cup Homemade Mayonnaise
1 tablespoon fresh basil, chiffonade,
  additional for garnish
1 tablespoon fresh chives, finely chopped,
  additional for garnish
1 tablespoon fresh mint, chiffonade,
  additional for garnish

1 tablespoon fresh chervil, chiffonade
  (if chervil not available, just omit)
3 cups panko (Japanese breadcrumbs)
1 cup rice flour (found in the international
  section of the grocery store)
1 tablespoon baking powder
1 teaspoon cayenne pepper
¾-1 cup club soda, chilled
Canola oil for frying
Bean sprouts and micro-greens for garnish

~

A mango has one large seed in the center of the fruit. Place the mango with the narrow side facing up. Starting ¼-inch from the stem, slide the knife along each side of the pit to cut off the "cheeks." Peel skin from the cheeks and remove the flesh. Repeat on the other side and remove both small strips of flesh remaining on the seed. Cut the mango flesh from the skin and place in a blender. Add lime juice and blend until smooth. Season to taste with salt. Refrigerate until ready to serve.

Pick through the crab meat and discard any shell or cartilage. In a large bowl, combine the red pepper, mayonnaise, basil, chives, mint and chervil. Stir in ½ cup panko and gently fold in the picked crab meat. (The crab mixture should be wet enough to hold together.) Add a little more mayonnaise, if needed. Shape the crab mixture into 3-inch cakes and chill until firm.

In a medium bowl, whisk rice flour with baking powder and cayenne. Whisk in ¾ cup club soda, adding more as needed to form a batter. Place remaining 2½ cups panko in a shallow dish. Dip the crab cakes into the batter and then into panko to coat.

Heat a large cast iron skillet and fill with 1 inch of oil. Heat oil to 375°. Fry crab cakes until golden brown, about 3 minutes per side. Place on a paper towel lined plate to drain and keep warm until ready to serve.

To serve, place ¼ cup mango puree in center of each plate, top with crab cakes and garnish with bean sprouts and micro-greens.

HOMEMADE MAYONNAISE

2 large egg yolks
3 tablespoons freshly squeezed lemon juice
2 tablespoons Dijon mustard
1 teaspoon cayenne (more to taste)
2 cups olive oil
Kosher salt to taste

~

Place yolks, lemon juice, Dijon mustard and cayenne in a blender and turn to high. Slowly drizzle in the olive oil until a thick emulsion forms. Taste and add salt and cayenne as needed. (This mayonnaise should be very strong in Dijon mustard and cayenne flavor.)

"My favorite vacation spot is St. George, Florida. It's dog-friendly, plus it's the beach and the oysters!"

Shrimp Lollipops

{ Serves 8 }

1 pound shrimp, peeled, deveined and finely chopped
2 tablespoons freshly grated ginger
2 tablespoons finely chopped green onion
½ teaspoon finely chopped fresh jalapeño
2 tablespoons finely chopped fresh mint
2 tablespoons finely chopped fresh basil
2 tablespoons finely chopped fresh cilantro
Sea salt and freshly ground white pepper
8 spring roll wrappers, thinly sliced
Skewers
Mae Ploy sweet chili sauce (found at Asian markets)

~

Place the shrimp in a large bowl, season with salt and white pepper. Add the ginger, scallion, jalapeño, mint, basil and cilantro and mix well. To test for seasoning, heat a sauté pan on medium-high heat, roll 1 tablespoon of the mixture into a ball and sauté until cooked through, about 3 minutes. Taste and adjust seasoning as needed. Scoop the shrimp into 1-inch balls and place on a rimmed baking sheet. Take 4 ribbons of spring roll wrapper and form a little nest. Place a shrimp ball in the nest and wrap completely to cover all sides. The wrapping will be a bit loose, this is fine. Return to the baking sheet and refrigerate about 1 hour or until chilled.

Heat a Dutch oven with 2 inches oil to 375°. Fry a few shrimp balls at a time until golden brown, about 3 minutes each. Remove to a paper towel lined plate to drain. Repeat, making sure the fryer oil is brought to 375° before adding new shrimp. Skewer each ball to make a lollipop and serve with the sweet chili sauce.

WHAT TO DRINK

Fun spirited flavors with a bit of spice tend to do well with Alsace's Gewürztraminers. Long considered sweet, the wines tend to be dry with wild aromatics and spice on the palate.

was born in Milwaukee, Wisconsin and came to Atlanta in 1995 after working in San Francisco and New York City. "I consider myself a Southern girl now—with a little New York attitude!" Sheri's meals growing up consisted of shake and bake pork chops with baked potatoes and spaghetti or chili in the crockpot, but always included fresh veggies from the garden. "I've always wanted to cook. It was a combination of my dad's best friend being a chef at a German restaurant, having a garden growing up and home economics class—it all just clicked!"

What are you scared of?
I start getting really nervous when my employees are late.

Who has provided the most inspiration to you and your career?
Sanford D'Amato and Eric Ripert. They taught me about the marriage of food, quality ingredients and being innovative.

If you could have any other job for a day, what would it be?
Sometimes, I'll be driving past the park and wish to be the guy riding on the lawnmower.

What's your favorite drink?
Mama Tini, the bartenders at Dish created it for me. It's Absolut Citron vodka, fresh lemon juice and Chambord.

Who's the most famous person you've cooked for?
Ivana Trump at the Quilted Giraffe and a New Year's Eve party for Elton John.

What's the weirdest ingredient you've ever used in a dish?
Baby eels at Le Bernardin. They're about an inch long and look like a zillion little worms.

What's your most used quote in the kitchen?
"Solo! Solo!" For dishes going out by themselves.

What's your favorite book?
Culinary Artistry.

TODD ANNIS

BOLD AMERICAN CATERING

Girls' Night In

Tuna Coronets

Field Green Salad with Strawberries, Praline Pecans
and Peppercorn Vinaigrette

Seared Diver Scallops with Grapefruit Gastrique

Petite Filet Mignon with Fingerling Potatoes

Oreo Truffles

Tuna Coronets

{ Makes 36 }

36 wonton wrappers
1 tablespoon dark sesame oil, additional for brushing the wontons
1 pound very finely diced sushi-grade yellow fin tuna
1 lime
2 teaspoons finely chopped shallot
2 teaspoons finely chopped garlic
2 teaspoons finely grated fresh ginger
¼ cup finely chopped chives
Kosher salt and freshly ground pepper

~

Heat the oven to 350°. Lightly brush both sides of the wonton wrappers with sesame oil. Wrap each wrapper around a small (4-inch) cone mold to form a cone. Place, wide side down, on a rimmed baking sheet. Repeat with remaining wrappers. Bake until crispy, about 12 minutes. Transfer to a rack to cool.

Place the tuna in a medium bowl. Zest the lime with a fine microplane grater. Add the lime zest, shallots, garlic, ginger, chives and 1 tablespoon dark sesame oil to the tuna. Season with salt and pepper and fold to combine. Just before serving, fold in the lime juice. Taste and adjust for seasoning with salt and pepper. Spoon the tuna into the cones and serve immediately.

"Food and the kitchen are focal points when you get together with friends. It's easy to have everyone participate when little bites are served rather than a large meal like Thanksgiving."

Field Green Salad with Strawberries, Praline Pecans and Peppercorn Vinaigrette

{ Serves 6 }

8 ounces mixed field greens
3 thinly sliced scallions
6 large strawberries, diced
1 cup Praline Pecans
¾ cup Peppercorn Vinaigrette
Kosher salt and freshly ground pepper

~

Combine the field greens, scallions, strawberries, and praline pecans in a large bowl. Add just enough vinaigrette to lightly coat the leaves; toss to combine. Season with salt and pepper and serve immediately.

PRALINE PECANS

½ cup granulated sugar
2 tablespoons water
1 cup pecans

~

Line a baking sheet with a non-stick silicone baking sheet and set aside. In a small skillet, stir sugar and water together and bring to a boil. Cook over medium-high heat, gently swirling pan until mixture begins to caramelize (turn brown) around the edges, about 4 minutes. With a fork, quickly stir the pecans in the sugar syrup until well coated and remove from the heat. Spread pecans on the prepared baking sheet and cool to room temperature. Remove to a cutting board and cut into bite sized pieces. Store pecans in an airtight container.

PEPPERCORN VINAIGRETTE

¼ cup granulated sugar
¼ cup balsamic vinegar
¼ cup unseasoned rice vinegar
2 tablespoons freshly cracked black peppercorns
1¼ cup canola oil

~

In a small saucepan over medium heat combine the sugar, balsamic vinegar, rice vinegar and peppercorns. Stir until sugar dissolves, 2-3 minutes. Remove from the heat. Gradually whisk in the oil. Set aside. (It will separate so it will be necessary to whisk it again before dressing the salad.)

Seared Diver Scallops with Grapefruit Gastrique

{ Serves 4 }

1 cup sugar
½ cup rice vinegar
2 Ruby Red grapefruits, juiced (or 1 cup unsweetened pink grapefruit juice)
1 tablespoon canola oil
Sea salt and freshly ground white pepper
12 large diver sea scallops, dry packed

~

In a 2-quart saucepan, combine sugar, vinegar and 1 cup grapefruit juice. Bring mixture to a boil. Reduce heat and simmer until the mixture is reduced by half and has a syrupy consistency, about 20 minutes.

Heat a large sauté pan over medium-high heat. Add canola oil and swirl to coat the bottom of the pan. Season both sides of the scallops with salt and pepper. When the pan is hot but not smoking, add the scallops and sear until crisp and golden, about 2 minutes per side. Remove to a paper towel lined plate to drain.

To serve, divide scallops between 4 warm plates. Drizzle with the grapefruit gastrique, sprinkle with sea salt and garnish with grapefruit sections. The bitter and acid of the grapefruit mixed with the sugar and the sweetness of the scallops is a perfect pair. The addition of the sea salt balances the dish perfectly.

Petite Filet Mignon with Fingerling Potatoes

{ Serves 4 }

1 pound fingerling potatoes
4 4-ounce beef tenderloin filets
Kosher salt and freshly ground pepper
4 tablespoons unsalted butter, divided
2 tablespoons olive oil
2 ounces cheese, such as white cheddar, goat cheese, or Roquefort
2 tablespoons sour cream
4 slices bacon, cooked crisp and crumbled
1 tablespoon finely chopped fresh chives

~

Preheat the oven to 425°. Rinse the fingerling potatoes and place directly on oven rack. Bake for 15-20 minutes or until fork tender.

Season both sides of the filets with salt and pepper. Heat a large ovenproof skillet over medium-high heat. Add 2 tablespoons butter and 2 tablespoons oil and heat until sizzling. Sear the filets on both sides, about 4 minutes per side. For rare, set aside on a warm plate to rest. For medium-rare, transfer to the oven until internal temperature reaches 140°, an additional 2-3 minutes.

Remove the potatoes from the oven and place on a warm platter. Split the fingerling potatoes lengthwise and pinch the ends to open the middle, like a crown. Season with salt and pepper and top potatoes with remaining 2 tablespoons butter, grated or crumbled cheese, sour cream, bacon bits and chives. To serve, divide the steaks and potatoes between 4 warm plates and serve immediately.

"When my family relocated to Atlanta in 1981, it was my first time living in a city that had a football team. I've had season tickets to the Falcons for five years."

Oreo Truffles

{ Makes 32 truffles }

4 ounces cream cheese, softened
2 cups crushed Oreo cookies, about 18 cookies
2 cups chocolate chips

~

In the bowl of a stand mixer fitted with the paddle attachment, beat cream cheese on high speed until fluffy. Add the crushed cookies and beat on low speed until well combined. Refrigerate this mixture for 2 hours. Line a rimmed baking sheet with waxed or parchment paper. Scoop out heaping teaspoons of the mixture and roll into about 1-inch balls with your hands (wear latex gloves for easy clean up) and place on prepared pan.

In a 3-quart saucepan, heat 2 cups of water to a simmer. Place the chocolate chips in a medium-sized metal bowl that will sit safely on the pan. Place the bowl on top of the pan to create a double boiler. Allow the chips to slowly melt, gently stirring, until there are no lumps. One at a time dip the Oreo balls into chocolate and, using two small spoons, rotate back and forth, until the Oreo balls are completely coated. Place back onto parchment. Repeat until all Oreo balls are coated with the chocolate. Place tray of truffles in the refrigerator for at least 45 minutes to allow the outer coating to harden.

WHAT TO DRINK

As the ladies arrive, be sure to have a thirst quenching white that can lead into the courses ahead. Austrian Grüner Veltliner's minerality, refreshing palate, and signature hint of white pepper make for quite a refreshing crowd pleaser.

Keep the Grü-Ve, what this trendy elixir has been dubbed, going until you reach the filet. While you sip on the white, allow a regal Cabernet Sauvignon to breathe. Once the beef comes around, you will relish the wait.

TODD ANNIS

admits to having become a chef so that he wouldn't starve. "My meals at home growing up were the worst. We ate cheap steak, plain baked potatoes and corn on the cob three nights a week for 15 years."
The first dish Chef Todd learned how to cook was Kraft Mac 'N Cheese.
"I still have the recipe memorized!"

What's the strangest thing that's ever happened on the job site?
I was cooking for a sports-oriented bar mitzvah where they gave away footballs, baseballs and basketballs. The guests ended up throwing the balls in the parking lot and busted all the windows of the cars at the restaurant.

What other jobs have you had?
I sold electronics and taught at The Art Institute of Atlanta.

What are your fondest childhood memories?
From going to Epcot and Disneyland. I really liked all the different countries and the rides, of course.

What's your most used quote in the kitchen?
"Sexy food." We're always making sure the food looks good and tastes good. Plus, it's just fun to say.

What words do you live by?
It's what you do in the time you have that makes a difference.

What song never gets old for you?
"Free Fallin'" by Tom Petty.

What's your favorite book?
The Lord of the Rings by J.R.R. Tolkien.

Who has provided the most inspiration to you and your career?
Chef Kevin Duffy. He inspired me to do the best I could not only for myself but for those around me.

JOËL ANTUNES

{ JOËL }

Gourmet Night

—

Gazpacho with Tomato Sorbet

Tuna Tartar with Pickled Daikon and Avocado Sorbet
with Pineapple Jus

Carrot Tortellini with Carrot-Mustard Sauce

Seared Scallops with Leek and Ricotta Tortellini

Hazelnut Chocolate Mille-feuille

Gazpacho with Tomato Sorbet

{ Serves 8 }

10 ripe Roma tomatoes, seeded and diced
½ cup water
3 small cloves garlic, gently crushed but intact, divided
2 tablespoons plus 2 teaspoons sugar, divided
2 tablespoons kosher or sea salt
½ teaspoon freshly ground pepper
20 fresh basil leaves, gently crushed, divided
2 cups red bell peppers, seeded and sliced thin
1 cup cucumber, peeled, seeded and sliced thin
6 slices white bread, crusts removed
1 cup extra virgin olive oil
⅓ cup sherry vinegar
Tomato Sorbet
Micro basil or 8 leaves basil, thinly sliced for garnish

~

Fill the bottom of a double boiler with 3 inches water and bring to a boil. Reduce the heat so the water is at a simmer. In the top of the double boiler, combine the tomatoes, ½ cup water, 1 clove garlic, 2 tablespoons sugar, 1 tablespoon salt, pepper and 5 basil leaves. Cook at a gentle simmer until thickened, about 2 hours, taking care that the water in the double boiler does not evaporate.

Remove the garlic clove and basil leaves from the tomato mixture and discard. Strain the tomato mixture through a coffee filter lined colander placed over a large bowl. This will take about 4 hours. Do not press on the tomatoes but let them drip naturally. This liquid is the tomato water, reserve for later use.

Pass the drained, cooked tomatoes through a food mill or pulse in a food processor to create a pulp for the gazpacho.

In a large non-reactive glass or stainless steel bowl, combine 1½ cups tomato pulp (reserve remaining for another use), ¼ cup tomato water (reserve remaining for another use), peppers, cucumber, remaining 2 cloves garlic, remaining 15 basil leaves, bread, remaining 1 tablespoon of salt, remaining 2 teaspoons sugar, oil and vinegar. Marinate overnight. Remove basil and garlic and discard. Purée in a blender until smooth, about 2-3 minutes. Strain through medium-holed strainer. (If too thick, add more tomato water to correct consistency.)

To serve, ladle gazpacho into a chilled soup plate. Top with a 1-ounce scoop of tomato sorbet. Garnish with micro basil or a chiffonade of fresh basil.

TOMATO SORBET

{ Makes 2½ cups }

10 ripe Roma tomatoes, seeded and puréed
²/₃ cup water
¼ cup sugar
2 teaspoons light corn syrup
1 teaspoon celery salt
Dash Tabasco hot sauce
⅓ cup sherry vinegar
¼ teaspoon lemon juice

~

Place tomato puree in a large, heavy-bottom, non-reactive or stainless steel pot. Add water, sugar and corn syrup and stir to combine. Bring to a boil over high heat. Remove from heat and cool.

Combine 2 cups of the cooked tomato pulp, celery salt, hot sauce, sherry vinegar and lemon juice in a blender and purée. Strain through a fine mesh strainer. Chill and freeze in an ice cream freezer, following manufacturer's instructions. When sorbet is finished, remove from machine and place in a container with a tight fitting lid. Freeze for 2-4 hours before serving. This is best served within 24 hours.

"I would go crazy without cycling. The Tour de France rode in front of my house when I was growing up. I need it."

Tuna Tartar with Pickled Daikon and Avocado Sorbet with Pineapple Jus

{ Serves 6 }

TUNA TARTAR

1 pound sushi-grade tuna
2 tablespoons fresh chives, minced
1 tablespoon preserved lemon
Dash Tabasco
1 tablespoon yuzu juice ("0" yuzu vinegar can be substituted)
2 tablespoons extra virgin olive oil
1 teaspoon sea salt
¼ teaspoon freshly ground pepper

~

Finely dice tuna and place in a bowl over ice. Gently fold in chives. Remove pulp and pith from the preserved lemon and finely mince the preserved lemon peel. Gently fold the lemon, hot sauce, yuzu juice, olive oil, salt and pepper into the tuna. Taste and adjust seasoning as needed.

PICKLED DAIKON

1 daikon
2 tablespoons salt
2 tablespoons sugar
½ cup honey
1 small sprig of rosemary
¼ cup champagne vinegar
¾ cup grapeseed oil
Kosher salt and freshly ground pepper

~

Peel the daikon and slice into very thin, almost paper thin rounds. Bring a small pot of water to a boil, add salt and sugar and return to the boil. Blanch daikon for 5 seconds and immediately shock in a bowl of water and ice. Remove from the ice bath and drain on paper towels to dry.

Combine honey and rosemary and bring to a boil, remove from heat and let steep 5 minutes. Remove rosemary and whisk in vinegar. While whisking continuously, slowly drizzle in olive oil. Add dry daikon and marinate for at least 6 hours.

AVOCADO SORBET

1 cup filtered or bottled water
⅓ cup sugar
2 tablespoons corn syrup
2 ice cubes
3 medium ripe avocados
¼ cup plus 3 tablespoons freshly squeezed lime juice, strained

～

In a small saucepan, bring water and sugar to a boil and stir until sugar completely dissolves. Remove from the heat and stir in corn syrup and ice cubes; set aside to cool.

In a blender, purée avocado and lime juice until very smooth. Add cooled sugar water and blend. Freeze in ice cream freezer according to manufacturer's instructions. When the ice cream is ready, remove from the machine and pack in an airtight container. Place in freezer to set. This is best used about 3 hours after making and should be used on the same day.

PINEAPPLE JUS

1 fresh pineapple (Maui Gold preferred)
½ vanilla bean

～

Peel and core the pineapple. Chop into large cubes and purée in blender for 2-3 minutes. Strain through coffee filter, do not press (this will take about 4 hours). Place strained pineapple juice in a small saucepan and bring to a boil, reduce heat to a low boil and reduce juice by 25 percent, skimming foam as it comes up. This should take about 15 minutes.

Remove from the heat. Split vanilla bean in half lengthwise and, with the tip of a paring knife, scrape seeds from inside of half the pod. Add the vanilla seeds to the pineapple jus and stir to combine.

To serve, remove daikon from marinade and pat dry. Arrange daikon in single layer in a 5-inch circle on serving plate. Place a 3-inch ring mold on top of daikon, press 1-inch layer of tuna into the mold and press with a spoon to even out. Carefully remove the mold. Top tuna with a small scoop of avocado sorbet and drizzle all with pineapple jus.

"No matter where I eat, Mom's roast chicken with tomato and an apple pie are always the best."

Carrot Tortellini with Carrot-Mustard Sauce

{ Serves 6 to 8 }

3 cups Delverde "00" soft wheat flour
1½ teaspoons salt
1¼ cups egg yolks (about 15 yolks)
1 large egg
1 tablespoon olive oil
Carrot Filling
Egg wash (1 egg yolk and 1 tablespoon water lightly beaten)

~

Put flour and salt in bowl of food processor fitted with a metal blade; blend for 15 seconds. With machine on, add yolks, egg and oil. When dough starts to form a ball take out and finish kneading by hand. Wrap in plastic and let rest in refrigerator for 30 minutes.

Set up a pasta rolling machine in an area with plenty of counter space. Dust the counter and pasta machine with flour. Set the machine rollers to the widest setting. Cut the chilled dough into 3 equal parts and keep the pieces that you are not working with covered. With your floured hands, press the first piece of dough into a rectangle flat enough to get one end to catch through the rollers. Roll the dough through on the first (widest) setting one time, fold the rolled dough in half lengthwise and roll through first setting again. Dust with flour as necessary and run the dough through the machine, changing the setting each time to roll thinner and thinner starting at 1 going through about 7 or 8. Once the dough has been through all settings you should have a piece of dough about 2-feet long.

Cut pasta sheets into 2-inch rounds. Brush outside edges with egg wash. Place a small spoonful of the carrot filling in the upper center of the pasta, fold and seal in a half moon shape. Fold again around fingers to form the tortellini. Seal with egg wash.

CARROT FILLING

1 pound organic carrots, peeled and diced (about 6 carrots)
14 tablespoons (1¼ sticks) unsalted butter
1 teaspoon salt
¼ teaspoon freshly ground pepper
¼ teaspoon toasted and ground cumin seed

~

Place carrots in a heavy-bottom saucepan, add water, just enough to cover carrots. Bring to a boil and cook until fork tender, about 12 minutes. While carrots are cooking, brown the butter. Place butter in a small saucepan over low heat. Heat until the butter turns a light brown and has a nutty fragrance. Skim off any foam and strain to remove any browned bits in the bottom. When carrots are cooked, drain and pat dry; spread on baking sheet and put in 200° oven until completely dry, about 20 minutes. Purée carrots with brown butter in blender while still hot. Add salt, pepper and cumin. Taste and adjust seasoning as needed. Cool.

CARROT-MUSTARD SAUCE

2 tablespoons unsalted butter
4 peeled and finely diced carrots
1 tablespoon granulated sugar
1 teaspoon kosher salt
¼ teaspoon freshly ground pepper
1 pinch toasted and ground cumin seed
½ clove garlic, crushed
1 teaspoon mustard seeds
2 cups vegetable stock
⅓ cup carrot juice
1½ cups heavy cream

4 threads saffron
1 pinch turmeric
1 pinch Madagascar curry powder
1 tablespoon finely chopped fresh parsley
2 teaspoons chiffonade of fresh tarragon
2 tablespoons Maille brand Dijon mustard
¼ teaspoon freshly grated orange zest
2 tablespoons unsalted butter
Kosher or sea salt and fresh finely ground pepper to taste

~

Heat a medium saucepan over medium heat. Add butter and swirl to melt. Add carrots and cook until soft, about 8 minutes. Add sugar, salt, pepper, cumin, garlic, mustard seeds, stock and carrot juice. Bring to a boil. Using an immersion blender, purée the mixture. Bring to a boil and reduce mixture by half, about 5 minutes. Add cream and reduce again by half, about 8-10 minutes. Add a pinch each of saffron, turmeric and curry and simmer for 15 minutes. Strain mixture and return to a boil. Remove from the heat, add parsley, tarragon and mustard and whisk to combine. Whisk in zest and butter, taste and adjust seasoning as necessary. Serve warm over tortellini.

To serve, cook tortellini in salted boiling water about 4 minutes or until cooked through and floating. Remove from cooking water with slotted spoon. Place 6 tortellini in a warm pasta bowl and top with the carrot/mustard sauce. Garnish with a sprig of tarragon and parsley.

Seared Scallops with Leek and Ricotta Tortellini

{ Serves 4 }

1¾ cups "00" flour (soft wheat White Lily flour can be substituted)
½ teaspoon salt
5 egg yolks
2 tablespoons water
3 tablespoons milk
Leek/Ricotta Filling
1 egg yolk lightly beaten with 1 tablespoon water for egg wash
Browned Butter Sauce
16 large diver sea scallops, dry packed
3 tablespoons clarified butter
Fleur de sel
Optional garnish: freshly shaved truffles

~

Place flour and salt in food processor fitted with metal blade. Pulse to mix. Mix egg yolks, water and milk together. With processor running, slowly add the egg mixture to the flour through the feed tube and run just until the mixture starts to form a ball. Remove from processor and knead by hand until the dough is together in a ball. Pat the dough into a round disk and wrap with plastic wrap. Let rest for one hour. While the dough is resting, make the leek/ricotta filling.

Set up a pasta rolling machine in an area with plenty of counter space. Dust the counter and pasta machine with flour. Set the machine rollers to the widest setting. Cut the chilled dough into 3 equal parts and keep the pieces that you are not working with covered. With your floured hands, press the first piece of dough into a rectangle flat enough to get one end to catch through the rollers. Roll the dough through on the first (widest) setting one time, fold the rolled dough in half lengthwise and roll through first setting again. Dust with flour as necessary and run the dough through the machine, changing the setting each time to roll thinner and thinner starting at 1 going through about 7 or 8. Once the dough has been through all settings you should have a piece of dough about 2-feet long. Cut into 2-inch rounds. Lightly brush the outside edges of each round with the egg wash. Place 1 teaspoon filling onto each round, fold in half, press to seal and twist and tuck edges in to meet to form the tortellini. Cover with a piece of waxed paper until ready to serve. (If preparing more than a day in advance, blanch the tortellini for 1 minute in gently boiling salted, oiled water, shock in ice water, drain and freeze until ready to use.)

Heat a large sauté pan over medium-high heat. Add clarified butter and heat through. Season both sides of the scallops with salt and finely ground black pepper. Add the scallops and brown on both sides. When you turn the scallops, spoon the butter over top to braise. Cook just until firm, about 3 minutes per side.

In a large pot, boil 1 gallon water with 1 tablespoon salt. Drop the pasta in and gently boil until cooked through and floating, about 4 minutes. Remove with a slotted spoon and drain.

To serve, place 6 tortellini in a pasta or soup plate, top with 4 scallops and generously add brown butter sauce. Top with fresh sliced truffles and finish with a pinch of fleur de sel.

LEEK/RICOTTA FILLING

2 teaspoons olive oil
1 cup finely diced leeks (white part only), about 2 leeks
½ cup (4 ounces) whole milk ricotta cheese
1 teaspoon extra virgin olive oil
⅓ cup finely grated Parmigiano-Reggiano cheese

~

Heat a medium sauté pan over medium heat. Add olive oil and swirl to cover the bottom. Add leeks and cook until soft, adjusting the heat lower if leeks begin to color. When leeks are very soft, about 20 minutes into cooking, remove from heat and spread on a sheet pan to cool. When leeks are cooled, fold into ricotta cheese. Stir in olive oil and parmesan cheese. Chill until ready to use.

BROWNED BUTTER SAUCE

12 tablespoons (1½ sticks) unsalted butter
3 tablespoons chicken stock
1½ teaspoons red wine vinegar
3 cups finely grated Parmigiano-Reggiano (6 ounces)
1½ teaspoons olive oil
1 tablespoon whipped heavy cream

~

Place butter in a small saucepan over low heat. Heat below a simmer, just until the butter turns a light brown and has a nutty fragrance. Skim off any foam and strain to remove any browned bits in the bottom. Allow browned butter to cool. In a blender, blend the room temperature browned butter with the stock and vinegar until the sauce thickens and emulsifies. While the blender is running, add Parmigiano-Reggiano, olive oil and whipped cream. Purée. Keep warm until ready to serve.

Hazelnut Chocolate Mille-feuille

{ Serves 4 }

½ cup shelled and skinned hazelnuts
½ cup granulated sugar
¼ teaspoon salt
1¾ cups flour, additional for dusting
8 tablespoons (1 stick) unsalted butter, chilled, cubed
3 large egg yolks, lightly beaten
2 cups heavy whipping cream, divided
½ vanilla bean
5 ounces 65% bittersweet chocolate, chopped
3 ounces milk chocolate, chopped
3 tablespoons confectioners' sugar, additional for garnish
Chocolate Ice Cream

~

Place the hazelnuts, sugar, salt, and flour in a food processor fitted with a metal blade. Pulse in 30 second increments until the hazelnuts have processed into a powder. Add the cubed butter and pulse until the mixture resembles coarse meal. Some of the butter will still be in small, pea-sized pieces, which is desirable. Add the yolks and process just until the mixture comes together in a ball, about 45 seconds. Be careful not to over-process. Turn the dough onto clean surface and gather together in a ball. Pat flat, wrap with plastic wrap and refrigerate 4 hours or until firm.

Preheat oven to 350°. Line a rimmed baking sheet with a silicone baking mat (Silpat) and set aside. While the dough is chilling, make the chocolate cream.

Measure the 1 cup cream into a 2-cup glass measuring cup. Split the vanilla bean and, using the tip of a paring knife, scrape the beans from the pod and add to the cream. Place the scraped pod into the cream. Microwave the cream and vanilla until it comes to a boil. Remove from the microwave and stir in the bittersweet chocolate until completely melted and combined. Chill mixture until set, about 30 minutes. Remove the vanilla pod. Whip the chocolate cream with a handheld electric mixer just until fluffy.

Place the milk chocolate in a glass bowl and microwave on 50 percent power for 1 minute. Stir and repeat until the chocolate is melted and smooth. With an offset spatula, spread the milk chocolate in a very thin layer on a nonporous surface (marble or glass cutting board is ideal; alternately, you can wrap a wooden cutting board completely with plastic wrap). Cool to room temperature to set and cut into 4- x 2-inch rectangles (leaves). You will need 12 4- x 2-inch milk chocolate leaves.

Remove the now chilled dough from the refrigerator and unwrap. Lightly flour your clean work surface and place the chilled dough on the floured surface. Lightly dust the top of the dough with flour. With a rolling pin, roll the dough thin (about 2mm) and cut into 4- x 2-inch rectangles. Carefully place the cut dough onto the prepared baking sheet. Bake on center rack of oven at 350° for 10 minutes, or until golden around the edges. Remove from the oven and slide the baking mat onto a cooling rack.

In a chilled bowl, whip the remaining 1 cup cream with 3 tablespoons confectioners' sugar to firm peaks to make the chantilly cream. Set aside.

To serve, spread one hazelnut biscuit with chocolate cream, add a milk chocolate leaf, repeat with the chocolate cream and milk chocolate leaf. Add a layer of chantilly cream and top with a milk chocolate leaf. Place on serving plate, dust with confectioners' sugar and add one small scoop of chocolate ice cream.

CHOCOLATE ICE CREAM

1¼ cups whole milk
¾ cup heavy cream
¾ tablespoon corn syrup
3¼ ounces milk chocolate, chopped

~

In a small saucepan, bring milk and cream to a boil. Remove from the heat and stir in the corn syrup until well blended. Stir in the chocolate until completely melted. Chill mixture overnight. Freeze in an ice cream maker according to manufacturer's directions. Pack ice cream in an airtight container and freeze for 3-6 hours before serving. This is best if served on the same day it is frozen.

WHAT TO DRINK

Oregon's Pinot Noir has been lauded and compared to France's legendary red Burgundies, but less press has been afforded the state's white Pinot, Pinot Gris. That is starting to change, and there's no wonder why. The wines are sublime with delicate floral aromas giving way to light lemony flavors. Go all the way to dessert with an Oregon Pinot Gris. With the dessert, give Vin Santo a chance.

toyed with the idea of becoming a pilot or professional cyclist as a very young boy, but by the age of 14 he knew he wanted to pursue a culinary career. A prestigious list of international restaurants and hotels soon followed, leading him to Atlanta and his eponymous restaurant, JOËL. Cooking is but one of Antunes' passions. He rides his bike 35 to 50 miles a day and follows that by a quick 8 mile run. And that's an easy day! Look for him on the Silver Comet Trail around 7 A.M.

Q&A

What's the weirdest ingredient you've ever used in a dish?
A live turtle. I was at the Mandarin in Thailand and I told the guys in the kitchen to take it and do something with it!

What's your favorite drink?
Freshly squeezed orange juice. And of course, I love red wine.

What was the first dish you learned to cook?
An apple tart. My grandmother taught me.

Who's someone famous that you've cooked for?
I cooked Elizabeth Taylor's birthday dinner on Malcolm Forbes' yacht.

What would you do if you won the lottery?
I would give some of it to people I like. I wouldn't need it all. I like simple things. I would still work, but in a different way.

What's your favorite vacation spot?
When I was younger I went to crazy places like Mozambique, Congo, Pakistan, Angola, Burma. I was in those places when it was very dangerous and I thought it was great. Now, I'm happy to spend my vacation time in the south of France with my family and friends there.

Where do you eat when you're not at your restaurant?
Muss & Turner's, Watershed, Floataway Café.

PIERO PREMOLI

PRICCI

Il Menu Isole - Italian Coastal Dinner

Cappellacci

Burrata

Capesante

Tonno

Fragole

Cappellacci

{ Serves 6 }

¼ cup plus 1 tablespoon extra virgin olive oil, divided
½ pound fresh shrimp, shelled, deveined, and coarsely chopped
4 ounces sheep's milk ricotta
¼ cup breadcrumbs
2 ounces pecorino cheese, grated, plus additional for garnish
2 pounds Roma tomatoes (about 10 tomatoes)
½ cup finely diced shallots (about 4 shallots)
2 sprigs fresh thyme
Pasta Dough
2 tablespoons finely chopped scallions for garnish
Salt and freshly ground pepper to taste

~

In a 10-inch sauté pan, heat 1 tablespoon olive oil until it shimmers. Add the shrimp and sauté until they curl, turn pink, and are no longer translucent, about 3-4 minutes. Transfer the shrimp and cooking liquid to a bowl and chill. When the shrimp mixture is chilled, add the ricotta, breadcrumbs, grated pecorino and salt and freshly ground pepper to taste. Mix until well combined and store in refrigerator until ready to use.

In a 6-quart stock pot bring 4 quarts of water to a boil. With a paring knife, cut an "X" in the bottom of each tomato. Once the water is boiling, drop the tomatoes in a few at a time and leave them for 15-30 seconds or until you see the skin splitting. Remove the tomatoes from the boiling water and drop into a bowl of ice water to stop the cooking. Once the tomatoes are cool, pull the skin off with the tip of your knife and cut the tomatoes in half and remove seeds. Place the skins and seeds into a fine mesh strainer over a bowl and mash to render as much juice as possible. Finely dice the tomatoes.

Heat ¼ cup olive oil in a 3-quart saucepan over medium heat. Add the shallots and cook until tender, about 5-6 minutes. Add the finely diced tomatoes and rendered juice to the pan, turn the heat to low and simmer for 45 minutes. Add the thyme sprigs. Remove the sauce from the heat and add salt and pepper to taste. Keep warm until ready to serve.

Set up a pasta rolling machine in an area with plenty of counter space. Dust the counter and pasta machine with flour. Set the machine rollers to the widest setting. Cut the dough round into 3 equal parts and keep the pieces that you are not working with covered. With your floured hands, press the first piece of dough into a flat rectangle enough to get one end to catch through the rollers. Roll the dough through on the first setting one time, fold the rolled dough

"The role of the chef is looking and touching."

in half lengthwise and roll through first setting again. Dust with flour as necessary and run the dough through the machine, changing the setting each time to roll thinner and thinner starting at 1 going through about 7 or 8. Once the dough has been through all settings you should have a piece of dough about 2-feet long. Cut this piece into 4- x 4-inch squares. Remove the shrimp filling from the refrigerator and measure 1 tablespoon of filling into the center of each square, lightly pressing the filling down so as to be able to fold dough over it. Mix together the remaining egg with 1 teaspoon of water and beat lightly. Brush 2 sides of the square of pasta with the egg wash; fold the pasta over, corner to corner, to make a triangle, gently pressing out any air pockets as you go. Press and firmly seal edges together with your fingers. Place the stuffed pasta on a lightly floured rimmed baking sheet and cover with a tea towel while you repeat the process with the rest of the dough and filling. You should get 8 4- x 4-inch squares out of each section of dough, resulting in 24 pieces total.

Heat the tomato sauce and remove the thyme sprigs.

Bring an 8-quart stock pot with 6 quarts of water to a heavy, rolling boil. Add a pinch of salt and cook the pasta for 4-6 minutes or until it floats and is tender. Drain the pasta and toss with the warm tomato sauce. Serve 4 cappellacci per person with about ½ cup of sauce for each. Garnish with scallions and shaved pecorino.

PASTA DOUGH

1 cup all-purpose flour, additional for flouring
1 cup semolina flour, additional for dusting
1 teaspoon salt
4 large eggs, divided
2 tablespoons olive oil
1 teaspoon water

~

In the bowl of a stand mixer fitted with the paddle attachment, combine the all-purpose flour, semolina flour, salt, 3 eggs, and 2 tablespoons of olive oil and mix at medium speed for 2-3 minutes. If you do not have a stand mixer, this can be done in the food processor or by hand. Turn the dough out onto a floured surface and knead the dough for about 5 minutes or until it becomes elastic. Wrap the dough in plastic wrap and allow to rest for 30 minutes at room temperature.

Burrata

{ Serves 6 }

4 medium heirloom tomatoes, cut into wedges
½ cup extra virgin olive oil
¼ cup aged red wine vinegar
Kosher salt and freshly ground pepper
1 recipe Homemade Sardinian Flatbread or ½ pound of carta da musica flatbread
    or flat cracker bread
12 ounces of Burrata or fresh buffalo mozzarella, cut into wedges
¼ cup, tightly packed, coarsely chopped, fresh basil leaves

∽

Place the tomatoes, olive oil and vinegar in a bowl and toss to combine. Season with salt and pepper. Allow to sit at room temperature for 5-10 minutes for the flavors to blend. To serve, break one piece of the homemade Sardinian flatbread into 3-4 inch pieces and set in the center of each plate. Place 2 ounces Burrata on top of the bread. Arrange some marinated tomato wedges around the plate, dress each salad with liquid from tomatoes and garnish with chopped basil.

HOMEMADE SARDINIAN FLATBREAD

3 cups all-purpose flour, additional for flouring
2 teaspoons salt
1¼ ounce package active dry yeast
1 cup lukewarm water (100-110°)
1 tablespoon extra virgin olive oil, additional for brushing

∽

In small mixing bowl combine flour and salt. Put the water in a medium mixing bowl, sprinkle yeast over the water and allow to sit for 5 minutes. Once the yeast has dissolved, gradually stir in oil and 2¾ cups of the flour mixture with a spoon and then use your hands to bring together. Use the rest of the flour only if necessary to make workable dough. Turn the dough onto a floured countertop and knead 6-8 times or until it forms a ball. Place in an oiled bowl and loosely cover with plastic wrap and allow to rest at room temperature for 1½-2 hours, until doubled in bulk. Preheat oven to 450°. Cut the dough into 6 equal pieces. With a rolling pin, on a lightly floured surface, roll each piece into 8- x 10-inch rounds. Spray a baking sheet with non-stick spray and place 2 rounds per pan. Bake for 10 minutes, remove from oven, brush with some olive oil and bake for 3-5 minutes more or until crisp and golden brown. Allow to cool completely before cracking into pieces.

"I am more and more conscious about the food that I eat."

Capesante

{ Serves 6 }

1 pound 12 ounces heirloom tomatoes, coarsely chopped

¾ cup aged red wine vinegar, divided

1 ¼-ounce envelope unflavored gelatin

1 cup rinsed Quick Preserved Lemons or store-bought preserved lemons

¼ cup water

1 cup extra virgin olive oil, divided

12 ounces shelled fresh fava beans (if fava beans aren't available substitute frozen lima beans)

½ cup diced Vidalia onion (about ½ small onion)

2 tablespoons chopped fresh garlic

1 bunch fresh parsley, leaves picked and rinsed well

1-1½ pounds (approximately 18) George's Bank Sea Scallops (if these aren't available
    use large diver sea scallops, dry packed)

Kosher salt and freshly ground pepper

~

TOMATO GELATIN

In a medium sized mixing bowl combine the chopped tomatoes with a pinch of salt, a few grinds of fresh pepper and ¼ cup of the red wine vinegar. With a potato masher, or using a food mill with the largest holed insert, mash the tomatoes to release their juice. Place the pulp in a fine mesh strainer set over a bowl and cover with plastic wrap. Allow the tomatoes to drain for at least 8 hours or overnight. Once the tomatoes have drained, you should have about 1½ cups of tomato water. Place ½ cup of the tomato water in a small bowl and sprinkle the envelope of gelatin over top to soften. Put remaining 1 cup of tomato water into a small saucepan and bring to a boil then pour into bowl with the softened gelatin. Mix until the gelatin is dissolved. Pour into a shallow container, cover and refrigerate for at least 8 hours or until set. Once the gelatin has set, cut into ½-inch cubes.

PRESERVED LEMON EMULSION

In a food processor fitted with the metal blade, combine 1 cup rinsed quick preserved lemons or rinsed, sliced store-bought preserved lemons with ¼ cup of water, pulse to combine. With the machine running, slowly drizzle in ¼ cup of olive oil until mixture emulsifies. Put into an airtight container and store in the refrigerator until ready to serve.

MACCO DI FAVA

In a 6-quart stock pot, combine shelled beans, onion, and garlic. Cover with water and bring to a boil. Cover and reduce the heat to medium-low and cook for 15 minutes or until the beans are very soft. Drain and put into the bowl of a food processor fitted with the metal blade and pulse 5-6 times. Add the parsley and the remaining ½ cup red wine vinegar. With the machine running, slowly drizzle in ½ cup olive oil. Process this mixture until very smooth. Add salt and pepper to taste and keep warm or room temperature until ready to serve.

Season the scallops on both sides with salt and pepper. Heat a large cast iron or non-stick sauté pan over medium-high heat and add the remaining ¼ cup of olive oil. Once the oil is hot, just below the smoke point, add the scallops to the pan without overcrowding, working in batches as necessary. Sear for about 1-1½ minutes per side, until a golden crust forms on each side.

To serve, spread about ⅓ of a cup of the fava bean puree in the center of the plate, place 3 scallops on top of the puree and spoon some of the preserved lemon emulsion around the plate and over the scallops. Place 3-4 tomato gelatin cubes around the plate and serve.

QUICK PRESERVED LEMONS

{ Makes 1 cup }

2 lemons
½ cup sugar
½ cup salt

~

Slice the lemons about ⅛-inch thick, removing the seeds as you go. In a small bowl, combine the sugar and salt. In a shallow glass dish, layer the lemons with the sugar/salt mixture, repeating until all ingredients are in the bowl. Cover with plastic wrap and refrigerate for at least 24 hours and up to 1 week. Rinse under cold water before use.

"My three weeks of vacation are sacred. I usually spend a week visiting chef friends in Italy, a week sailing with family, and a week at the beach."

Tonno

{ Serves 6 }

2 large eggs
3-4 ice cubes
2 tablespoons dried lavender
1½ teaspoons chopped garlic (about 3 cloves)
2½ cups coarsely chopped chives
¼ cup water
¾ cup plus 2 tablespoons extra virgin
   olive oil, divided
2 cups fresh shelled English peas
1 pound white asparagus, tough ends
   trimmed, tips and tender stalks bias
   cut in ¼-inch pieces

1 cup diced red onion (about 1 medium)
½ cup vegetable stock
8 tablespoons unsalted butter, cut into
   pieces, divided
6 6- to 8-ounce, 1-inch fresh tuna steaks
½ cup all-purpose flour
¼ cup finely diced Calabrese chiles
   (jalapeño can be substituted)
1½ cups Marsala wine
Salt and freshly ground pepper to taste

~

Place eggs in a 1-quart saucepan, add enough water to cover. Bring to a boil and reduce heat to a simmer for 5 minutes. Remove from the heat and leave in the hot water for 3 minutes. Run under cold water just until cool enough to handle. Gently peel the soft boiled eggs and remove all shell. In a blender container, combine ice cubes, soft boiled eggs, lavender, garlic, chives, and ¼ cup water. Blend on medium-high speed and, with the machine running, slowly drizzle in ½ cup of the olive oil. The sauce will be thick and emulsified. Add salt and pepper to taste, cover and refrigerate until ready to use.

Fill a 4-quart pot three-fourths with water and bring to a boil. Add 1 tablespoon salt, return to a boil and add the peas, asparagus, and red onion. Return to a boil and cook for 4 minutes. Drain the vegetables in a colander and place the pot back on the heat. Add the vegetable stock, bring to a boil, remove from the heat and whisk in 6 tablespoons of butter until melted. Add the vegetables back to the pot and cover until ready to use.

In a large 12- to 14-inch heavy-bottom sauté pan, heat 3 tablespoons of olive oil over medium-high heat. Season the tuna on all sides with salt and pepper then dust all sides with flour, shaking off any excess. Place tuna steaks in the pan without crowding and cook for 2 minutes; flip and cook for 2 minutes for rare. Remove the tuna from the pan to a plate and cover with aluminum foil to keep warm. Work in batches and repeat until all tuna is cooked, adding more oil as needed. When all of the tuna is cooked, return the pan to high heat, add the chiles and cook for about 1 minute or until soft, stirring continuously. Add the Marsala and deglaze the pan, scraping up any browned bits from the pan into the sauce. Reduce the Marsala by half which will take about 4-5 minutes. Remove the pan from the heat and whisk in the remaining 2 tablespoons of butter until melted and the sauce has thickened a bit. Season with salt and pepper to taste.

To serve, divide the vegetables and a bit of butter sauce between 6 warmed plates. Cut each tuna steak on the diagonal and arrange atop the vegetables. Drizzle the tuna with the Marsala sauce and decoratively spoon the chive sauce around the plate.

Fragole

STRAWBERRIES DRIZZLED WITH LIMONCELLO SYRUP
IN AN ALMOND TUILLE BASKET WITH CHANTILLY CREAM

{ Serves 6 }

4 tablespoons (½ stick) unsalted butter, room temperature
¾ cup sugar, divided
¼ cup light corn syrup
½ cup finely chopped slivered almonds
½ cup all-purpose flour
⅛ teaspoon salt
½ cup limoncello or lemon liquor
½ cup water
1 cup heavy whipping cream
1 cup mascarpone
¼ cup confectioners' sugar, additional for garnish
½ vanilla bean
2 pints very ripe strawberries, washed, stems removed and diced
Zest of 3 lemons
2 tablespoons honey

~

Preheat oven to 325°.

In a 3-quart saucepan, bring butter, ¼ cup sugar, and corn syrup to a boil. Remove from the heat. Fold in almonds, flour, and salt. Mix until well combined. Allow the dough to cool at least 5 minutes. Line a baking sheet with a silicone baking mat, scoop a tablespoon of dough onto the mat and spread with the back of the tablespoon to a very thin 4-inch circle. Repeat until all dough is used. Bake for 12-13 minutes turning halfway through cooking time for even browning. Set up 6 small cups or a muffin tin upside down on the counter. Remove tuilles from the oven and allow to cool for about 30-45 seconds, just until you are able to remove from the pan with a very thin, flexible spatula. Quickly, but gently, lift the tuilles off the silicone baking mat and shape over the upside down cups and press gently to form a basket. Allow to cool completely. Repeat with remaining dough. This makes 12 tuilles. Store any unused tuilles in an airtight container. (continued on next page)

In a small saucepan, combine limoncello, remaining ½ cup sugar and ½ cup water and bring to a boil. Reduce by half to a syrup-like consistency. Remove from heat and allow the limoncello syrup to cool at room temperature until ready to use.

In a stand mixer fitted with the whisk attachment, combine cream, mascarpone and confectioners' sugar. Split half the vanilla bean and scrape the seeds with the tip of a knife and add to the cream mixture. Whip until medium peaks form. This will not take very long. Be careful not to over-whip. Cover and store in the refrigerator until ready to use.

In a medium bowl, toss strawberries with the lemon zest. Ten minutes before serving, add the limoncello syrup and toss.

To serve, place a teaspoon of chantilly cream in the middle of dessert plate. Place tuille basket on top of cream to secure it on the plate. Place a generous spoon of chantilly cream in the tuille and top with a generous spoon of the macerated strawberries, drizzle some of the limoncello syrup over the top. Garnish the plate with sifted confectioners' sugar and a drizzle of honey.

WHAT TO DRINK

No talk of the Italian coast can go on without mention of the Boot's most famous white, Pinot Grigio. These fruity whites definitely do the trick. If you are looking for a change, try the whites from the Campania region, home of Naples and famed for its mozzarella. Notable varietals are Falanghina, Fiano di Avellino, and Greco di Tufo.

PIERO PREMOLI

is a native of Milan, Italy. He arrived in the United States for the first time after a month-long transatlantic sailing excursion. Lovers of fine Italian cuisine are glad that he stayed on, serving as an executive chef for numerous restaurants including Donald Trump's Taj Mahal in New Jersey. A move to Atlanta in 2001 began his relationship with the Buckhead Life Restaurant Group which led to his 2005 appointment as executive chef at Pricci.

What restaurant do you dine in when not in your own?
JOËL.

Does your wife cook?
Yes, but I'm faster.

If you could have another job for a day, what would it be?
A professional sailor.

What's your favorite time of the day?
Sunset on vacation. After a day of sailing, you stop at the marina, open a bottle of white wine, relax on the cockpit, the salt's on your skin.

What's something you love to do?
Spend time with my daughter, Georgia.

What was the first dish you learned how to cook?
A panini. Growing up, we had a panini press in the family kitchen. You'd get home from school, put the ham and cheese in the bread and make a panini.

Who's a mentor of yours?
Pano Karatassos.

What is your favorite book?
The Name of the Rose by Umberto Ecco.

Where would you like to visit that you've never been?
Zanzibar. It has a cool name. And it's a tropical beach.

111

VIRGINIA WILLIS

Southern Evening Soirée
—

Onion Confit on Garlic Toasts

Classic Crab Cakes with Tarragon Crème Frâiche

Grits and Greens

Peach-Dijon Crusted Pork Tenderloin

Mocha Pots de Crème with Palmiers

Onion Confit on Garlic Toasts

{ Makes 2 cups }

1 baguette cut in ¼-inch slices
1 tablespoon extra virgin olive oil, plus additional for brushing
2 cloves garlic, papery skin removed
1 tablespoon unsalted butter
6 cups coarsely chopped onions (about 6 onions)
1 teaspoon sugar
1 teaspoon kosher salt
½ teaspoon freshly ground pepper
¼ cup red wine
1 tablespoon fresh thyme, chopped, plus additional for garnish
Kosher salt and freshly ground pepper to taste

Preheat oven to 325°. On a large baking sheet, arrange bread slices in one layer and lightly brush both sides of each slice with olive oil. Toast slices in middle of oven 15 minutes and turn over. Toast an additional 5 minutes, or until rich golden brown. Transfer toasts to a rack to cool. Cut the garlic in half lengthwise and rub the toasts with the cut side of the garlic. Let cool. (Toasts may be made 2 days ahead and kept in an airtight container at room temperature.)

Heat the butter and extra virgin olive oil in a 10-inch skillet over medium heat. Add onions and sugar. Season to taste with salt and pepper. Cook, stirring occasionally, until onions are soft, 15-20 minutes. Increase heat to medium-high. Add red wine and cook, stirring occasionally, until wine is completely reduced and onions are deep golden brown, another 15-20 minutes. Add the chopped thyme; taste and adjust for seasoning. Transfer onions to a small serving bowl, garnish with a sprig of thyme, and serve with toasts.

Classic Crab Cakes with Tarragon Crème Frâiche

{ Makes 24 bite size hors d'oeuvre }

1 pound lump crabmeat, picked over for cartilage and shell
1 large egg, lightly beaten
⅓ cup panko (Japanese breadcrumbs)
3 tablespoons mayonnaise
1 lemon, juice and zest
½ teaspoon Worcestershire sauce
Dash hot sauce, such as Tabasco
½ cup crème frâiche or sour cream
¼ cup freshly chopped tarragon, plus additional for garnish
Pinch of cayenne
¼ cup canola or peanut oil
Kosher salt and freshly ground pepper

In a large bowl, gently combine the crabmeat, egg, panko, mayonnaise, lemon juice and zest, Worcestershire sauce, hot sauce, salt, and pepper. The mixture will be fairly wet. Using a small ice cream scoop or tablespoon, form small crab cakes on a rimmed baking sheet. Refrigerate to chill and set, about 30 minutes.

In a small bowl, combine the crème frâiche and tarragon. Season with a pinch of cayenne, salt and pepper. Set aside.

Heat the oil in a large non-stick skillet over medium heat. Remove the crab cakes from the refrigerator and, with an offset spatula, gently transfer the cakes into the oil. Do not crowd the cakes, work in batches as necessary. Sauté until the crab cakes are golden brown and cooked through, 1-2 minutes per side. Remove the cakes from the skillet and place on a plate lined with paper towels to drain.

Transfer the cakes to a large serving platter. Using a piping bag fitted with a round tip or a small spoon, top each crab cake with a small dollop of the seasoned crème frâiche. Garnish each cake with a tarragon leaf. Serve immediately.

"I was the kid who had to take crêpes aux champignons to school for lunch."

Grits and Greens

{ Serves 4 to 6 }

2 tablespoons corn oil, preferably unrefined, divided
1 cup grated Vidalia onion (about 1 onion)
½ cup fresh corn kernels (about 1 ear)
3 cups water
1 cup whole milk
1 cup coarse-ground yellow grits or cornmeal
2 tablespoons unsalted butter
1 finely chopped clove of garlic
2 cups baby greens, such as kale or collards, trimmed, stemmed, and chiffonade*
Kosher salt and freshly ground pepper

~

Heat 1 tablespoon of the oil in a large saucepan over medium heat. Add the onions and cook until transparent, about 2 minutes. Add the corn and cook, stirring occasionally, until tender, about 5 minutes.

Increase heat to medium-high, add the water and milk, and bring to a boil. Whisk in the grits, reduce heat to low and simmer, stirring often, until thick, about 30 minutes. Add 2 tablespoons butter, season generously with salt and pepper, set aside and keep warm.

Heat the remaining tablespoon of oil in a large sauté pan over medium-high heat. Add the garlic and cook until fragrant, stirring constantly, 45-60 seconds. Add the greens and cook, stirring often, until wilted, 3-5 minutes. Add the wilted greens to the saucepan of grits and stir well to combine. Taste and adjust for seasoning with salt and pepper. Serve immediately.

* The technique for slicing the greens is known in French cooking as chiffonade. To chiffonade the stemmed greens, stack the leaves one on top of the other and roll tightly into a cylinder. Slice the cylinders of leaves crosswise into very thin strips. This technique may also be used with any leaves such as cabbage or basil.

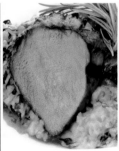

Peach-Dijon Crusted Pork Tenderloin

{ Serves 4 to 6 }

¾ cup brown sugar, firmly packed
¼ cup coarse kosher salt
2 cups boiling water
3 cups ice cubes
2 pork tenderloins
½ cup peach preserves
1 tablespoon finely chopped fresh rosemary leaves
½ cup Dijon mustard
Freshly ground pepper

~

Place the sugar and salt in a medium heatproof bowl. Pour the boiling water over the sugar mixture and stir to dissolve. Add the ice cubes and stir to cool. Add the tenderloins, cover the bowl and marinate, refrigerated, for 30 minutes. Remove the tenderloins from the brine, rinse thoroughly, and pat dry with paper towels.

In a small bowl, stir to combine the preserves, rosemary and mustard.

Season the tenderloins with pepper. Place tenderloins over a hot grill pan or on a preheated grill and grill for about 15 minutes or until the internal temperature reaches 130°. Brush with peach-mustard mixture until the temperature reaches 145°. Remove to a cutting board and cover with aluminum foil. Let the meat rest 5 minutes to allow the juices to redistribute. Slice on the diagonal, across the grain, and serve immediately.

"Once I was preparing grits for *Good Morning America* and stuffed tin foil in the bottom of the bowl to make it look full. When Joan Lunden went to spoon some out, I slapped her wrist and said 'don't touch the grits!'"

Mocha Pots de Crème with Palmiers

{ Serves 6 }

1 cup heavy cream
1 cup whole milk
5 ounces semisweet chocolate
1 tablespoon instant espresso or instant coffee powder
5 large egg yolks
⅓ cup granulated sugar
1 teaspoon vanilla extract
Pinch of fine sea salt
Approximately 4-6 cups of boiling water to create a bain marie (water bath)
Palmiers
Whipping cream, for garnish

~

Undeniably creamy and indulgent, these are the French version of pudding cups. Pots de crème are named such because of the traditional individually-lidded ceramic pots in which these custards are baked.

Place the oven rack in the lower third of the oven. Heat the oven to 325°. Place six 6-ounce pots de crème or ramekins in a medium roasting pan and set aside. Begin boiling water for a bain marie.

In a medium saucepan, combine cream, milk, chocolate, and espresso powder over medium heat. Bring almost to a simmer and remove from heat. Set aside, stirring occasionally, until chocolate is completely melted.

In a 1-quart measuring cup, whisk together the egg yolks and sugar. While whisking, add a little of the hot milk mixture to the egg mixture to temper (slowly bringing up the temperature of the egg mixture). Add the remaining milk mixture, and whisk to combine. Whisk in the vanilla and salt.

Pour approximately ½ cup of the egg mixture into each ramekin. Cover each of the ramekins tightly with aluminum foil to prevent a skin from forming. Fill pan with enough boiling water to come halfway up the sides. This is the bain marie. Carefully transfer the roasting pan to the oven. Bake until the custards are just set in the center, 35-40 minutes.

Remove the roasting pan from oven. Remove the pots from the water, and place on a wire rack to cool, about 30 minutes. When completely cooled, transfer to the refrigerator to chill completely, preferably overnight.

To serve, top with whipped cream and a palmier.

PALMIERS

{ Makes about 3½ dozen }

1 17¼-ounce package frozen puff pastry sheets (2 sheets), thawed
1 cup sugar, more if needed

~

On a work surface sprinkled with ¼ cup sugar, place one sheet puff pastry. Sprinkle top of sheet evenly with ¼ cup sugar. Using a rolling pin, roll the pastry sheet into a 12-inch square, pressing the sugar into both sides of the pastry.

Roll up one edge to middle of pastry sheet. Roll up parallel edge in same manner so that the two rolls are touching; press gently to seal roll. Repeat with remaining pastry and sugar. Wrap each roll tightly in plastic wrap and chill until firm, about 30 minutes. (Pastry rolls may be made 2 weeks ahead and frozen).

Preheat oven to 400°. Cut chilled pastry roll with a sharp knife crosswise into slices just under ¼-inch thick. (If roll is frozen, desired number of cookies may be cut frozen and the remaining log frozen again for later use.)

Place cookies 2 inches apart on an ungreased cookie sheet. Keep remaining pastry well chilled. Bake palmiers in batches in middle of oven until tops are golden brown. Using an offset spatula, turn and continue baking 10 minutes more or until golden brown. Transfer cookies to a rack to cool.

WHAT TO DRINK

As guests arrive treat them to a Southern classic, Mint Juleps, with the Onion Confit Toasts. Then segue into the wines.

A rich oaked Chardonnay from California is needed to stand up to the heady aromas of tarragon in the crab cakes. This wine can carry through the grits and greens.

As the plates are cleared from the grits, transition into a lush red to complement the pork. California and Chilean Merlot exhibit typical lush red fruit flavors with bold well-integrated tannins. Finish the evening with dessert and a small glass of a late harvest wine with honeysuckled character such as Montbazillac.

MINT JULEPS

4 cups sugar
4 cups water
Bunch of mint
Crushed ice
Kentucky bourbon

~

Mix the sugar and water in a saucepan. Heat and stir until fully incorporated. Allow to cool and refrigerate until cold.

While simple syrup chills, bruise bunch of mint in a wide-mouthed pitcher by pressing mint against bottom with the back of a wooden spoon.

Add chilled simple syrup to mint and refrigerate overnight.

To serve, fill high ball glasses with crushed ice. Fill half and half with the bourbon and mint syrup. Stir until glass frosts. Garnish with mint and serve.

VIRGINIA WILLIS

is more than a cook. She's a teacher, author, food stylist and television producer of cooking shows. She got her start as an apprentice to Nathalie Dupree, honed her attention to detail as the kitchen director for Martha Stewart Living Television and then traveled the world as executive producer for *Epicurious* on The Discovery Channel. She was a tester and editor for *The All New, All Purpose Joy of Cooking*, author of *Pasta Dinners 1, 2, 3*, and co-author of *Home Plate Cooking*. Her new book celebrates three generations of Southern cooking and the style she calls "Bon Appetit, Y'all."

What did you want to be when you grew up?
An Indian princess.

What is your favorite guilty pleasure?
Bacon.

What's your favorite movie?
Coal Miner's Daughter. My favorite line is when Sissy Spacek says: "I may be ignorant but I ain't stupid."

What were your meals at home like growing up?
My mother was an avid cook. We had old-fashioned Southern, but also Cajun and Creole because we were in Louisiana.

What is your favorite drink?
Bourbon.

What are the words you live by?
Season as you go.

What is something that people would be surprised to know about you?
I turn into a big ol' redneck at the Braves games.

If you won the lottery, what would you do with the money?
Pay off my debt then take a long trip to learn about food. I would definitely work. I'd be able to be better at it.

JAY SWIFT

RAINWATER

The Great Outdoors

—

Sweet Georgia Brown Steamed Shrimp with Bloody Mary Cocktail Sauce

Steamed Sweet Corn, Red Potatoes and Spring Vidalias

Baked Sweet Potatoes with Maple Butter and Nutmeg

Kamado Oven Ribeye Steaks and Portobello Mushrooms

Grilled Vine Ripened Vegetables with Aged Sherry Vinaigrette

Fresh Strawberries and Cream

Sweet Georgia Brown Steamed Shrimp with Bloody Mary Cocktail Sauce

{ Serves 6 }

½ cup chili sauce
½ cup ketchup
1 tablespoon prepared horseradish
1 lemon, juiced
¼ cup vodka
⅓ cup finely minced celery (about 2 stalks)
1 small, finely minced red onion
¼ teaspoon celery salt
1 dash Worcestershire sauce
Kosher salt and freshly ground pepper
1 12-ounce bottle Sweet Georgia Brown Ale, more for drinking
¼ cup cider vinegar
3 pounds Georgia white shrimp, in the shell
¼ cup Old Bay seasoning

~

In a medium mixing bowl, combine the chili sauce, ketchup, horseradish, lemon juice, vodka, celery, onion, celery salt and a dash of Worcestershire sauce. Stir with a spoon and mix well. Taste and adjust flavors as needed with additional horseradish, lemon juice and salt and pepper. Cover and refrigerate.

Place a steamer basket in the bottom of a heavy-bottom pan, pour in just enough beer to come below the basket and add the vinegar. Place over high heat, cover, and bring to a boil. Season the shrimp liberally with Old Bay and evenly spread in the steamer basket. Reduce the heat to medium-high and steam the shrimp for about 4-6 minutes or until curled and opaque/pink throughout. If the shrimp are stacked, give them a stir after a couple of minutes to even the cooking. When you check the shrimp for doneness, also check to make sure there's plenty of liquid remaining in the pan, adding more as needed. Carefully remove the steamer basket and pour onto a serving tray. Place in the center of the table and serve with the cocktail sauce and plenty of hand towels for your guests.

Steamed Sweet Corn, Red Potatoes and Spring Vidalias

{ Serves 6 }

6 ears fresh corn
12 Vidalia spring onions, outer skins removed, greens and roots trimmed
12 red "new" potatoes, halved

~

Place a steamer basket in the bottom of a heavy-bottom pan. Add just enough water to come almost to the bottom of the basket. Line the basket with the corn husks and place the ears of corn on top. Cover, place over medium-high heat, bring to a boil, reduce heat and steam for 10 minutes. At 10 minutes, remove the cover, check to make sure there's plenty of water below the steamer basket, adding water as needed. Remove the corn, add the potatoes, place the corn back in on top of the potatoes, cover, bring back to a boil and steam 20 more minutes. At 20 minutes, check the potatoes, they should be almost fork tender. Check the water level again and add the onions. Cover and steam until the potatoes and onions are very tender, another 10 minutes. Serve piping hot.

Baked Sweet Potatoes with Maple Butter and Nutmeg

{ Serves 6 }

6 large sweet potatoes, scrubbed
8 tablespoons unsalted butter, softened
2 tablespoons maple syrup
Kosher salt and freshly ground pepper
1 whole nutmeg

~

Bring the Kamado* oven to 350°. If using a conventional grill, heat to medium-high. Wrap the sweet potatoes loosely in aluminum foil and place around the perimeter of the grill grate. Close the top and roast the potatoes for 1 hour, or until fork tender.

In a small bowl with a spoon or fork, combine the butter with the maple syrup, salt and pepper and mix well.

When the potatoes are cooked through and soft, remove from oven, slit lengthwise down the middle and press to "crown." Top each potato with a dollop of maple butter and with a microplane or nutmeg grater, dust with fresh grated nutmeg just before serving.

*A Kamado oven is a ceramic barbecue grill similar to a "Big Green Egg." They hold temperature very well and will reach very high temperatures. Because the "oven" is ceramic on all sides, and the lid is as well, the temperature inside is very even. A Kamado oven can be used for grilling, smoking or as an oven with electric heat source.

Kamado Oven Ribeye Steaks and Portobello Mushrooms

{ Serves 6 }

4 cloves finely chopped garlic
¼ cup olive oil
2 tablespoons balsamic vinegar
¼ teaspoon finely chopped fresh thyme
6 large portobello mushroom caps, stems removed
6 1½-inch-thick ribeye steaks
Coarse sea salt and freshly ground pepper
2 tablespoons canola oil

~

Pile hardwood charcoal up in the center of the firebox of the Kamado oven. Light the charcoal, cover and set to medium draft, and bring to 500°. This will take about 25 minutes. If you are using a conventional grill, preheat the grill to high.

In a large mixing bowl, whisk together the garlic, olive oil, vinegar and thyme. Season with salt and pepper. Add the mushrooms and turn to coat. Let the mushrooms marinate for 1 hour. Place the mushrooms, gill side down, around the perimeter of the grill. Close and cook for about 4 minutes, turn and cook another 5 minutes. When the mushrooms are almost done they will be a bit flexible and will bend without breaking. Leave the mushrooms on the grill.

Season steaks on both sides and brush with oil, set aside. Increase the draft and bring the temperature of the oven to 600°. Place the steaks in the middle of the grill, on the hottest spot. Place the mushrooms on top of the steaks and close the top. Cook 4-5 minutes, meat should be charring and crusty on the bottom. Remove the mushrooms to a plate, turn the steaks over and continue cooking to desired doneness, another 3-4 minutes for rare (internal temperature of steak 130°) or 5-6 minutes for medium (155°). Remove steaks, top with a mushroom cap and serve immediately.

"I read about food a lot, and about Southern culture. I like to think of food as anthropology, as an extension of culture."

Grilled Vine Ripened Vegetables with Aged Sherry Vinaigrette

{ Serves 6 }

2 zucchini, bias cut ½-inch thick
12 spears asparagus, tough ends trimmed
2 red bell peppers, quartered, seeds removed
3 Vidalia onions, halved
3 ripe tomatoes, halved
¼ cup plus 2 tablespoons olive oil, divided
2 finely minced shallots
1 clove finely minced garlic
¼ cup sherry vinegar
Kosher salt and freshly ground pepper
Fresh herbs for garnish (thyme, basil, oregano, parsley)

~

Preheat grill to medium heat. Lightly brush the zucchini, asparagus, bell peppers, onions and tomatoes with oil, season with salt and pepper. Place on grill until they just begin to soften, about 8 minutes, turning once as needed.

While the vegetables are grilling, make the vinaigrette. In a small bowl combine the remaining ¼ cup olive oil, shallots, garlic, sherry vinegar, salt and pepper. Whisk and set aside. Arrange the vegetables on a serving plate, drizzle with the vinaigrette and garnish with the fresh herbs.

Fresh Strawberries and Cream

{ Serves 6 }

1 quart fresh strawberries
3 tablespoons granulated sugar
1 pint heavy cream

~

Rinse the strawberries, remove the stems and hull. If berries are large, cut in half or quarters. Place the berries in a large bowl and sprinkle with the sugar to release the juices. Give the berries a toss to combine. When ready to serve, top the berries with the cream and give them a quick stir.

WHAT TO DRINK

As temperatures rise and outdoor dining becomes a way of life, cold beer is essential. Pale ales showcase the hops of beer, while pilsners remind us all of the liquid's quaffability. Throw in easy going brown ale with its affable, malty personality and all guests will be pleased.

JAY SWIFT

started out in the restaurant business at the age of 14, and restaurant work financed his high school and college English education. After two and a half years, he followed his heart—and stomach— to a culinary apprenticeship in a Maryland restaurant. Swift began his career in some of the Northeast's finest dining rooms, including a position at the venerable Mayflower Hotel in Washington, D.C., and a spot in the kitchen of noted restaurateur Bob Kinkead's 21 Federal in the nation's capital.

Where would you like to visit that you've never been before?
The Mediterranean.

If you could have a theme song playing every time you walk into the kitchen, what would it be?
Johnny Cash's version of Sound Garden's "Rusty Cage."

What's the strangest food you've ever consumed, and where?
Monkfish liver at Soto.

Who are some famous people you've cooked for?
Steve Martin, Samuel L. Jackson, Dan Akroyd, Senator John Edwards, Tyra Banks, and Courteney Cox.

What's your favorite vacation spot?
Outer Banks, NC and New York City.

What's your favorite place to eat when you're not at your own restaurant?
My deck or dining room.

What's your favorite book?
Atlas Shrugged.

What's your favorite drink?
Pinot Noir from California or Oregon, beer from Belgium.

What was the first dish you learned how to cook?
Steak on the grill or steamed hard crabs.

What's something that people would be surprised to find out about you?
I love politics and history.

ANTHONY SANDERS

Day of the Dead Fiesta

Salsa Fresca

Ceviche Estilo Jalisco

Pozole de Calabaza con Carnitas

Pescado al Mojo de Cilantro

Pudin de Pan con Chocolate y Chile

Salsa Fresca

{ Makes 3 cups }

3 large ripe tomatoes, approximately 1½ pounds, cored and chopped
½ cup diced onion
1 finely chopped fresh jalapeño pepper
2 tablespoons finely chopped fresh cilantro
1 tablespoon freshly squeezed lime juice
1 tablespoon kosher salt

~

In a medium non-reactive glass or stainless bowl, combine the tomatoes, onion, jalapeño, cilantro, lime juice and salt. Cover loosely with plastic wrap and allow the salsa to marinate, at room temperature, for 30 minutes. (If very ripe tomatoes are not available use good quality canned tomatoes and decrease the lime juice.) Taste and adjust for seasoning with salt. Serve with tortilla chips, on quesadillas, or pour over eggs and bake for huevos rancheros.

"When I go out, people never believe that I'm a chef, they're always like, 'Man, you're too young, there's no way.'"

Ceviche Estilo Jalisco

JALISCO STYLE CEVICHE

{ Makes 4 to 6 appetizer portions }

½ pound tilapia filet, trimmed and cut into ¼-inch dice
1 cup plus 2 tablespoons freshly squeezed lime juice, divided
¼ cup chopped green onions
2 tablespoons diced red bell pepper
2 tablespoons diced yellow bell pepper
¼ cup finely chopped fresh cilantro (approximately ½ bunch)
1 finely chopped pickled jalapeño
1¼ teaspoons kosher salt
Tortilla chips, for serving

~

Combine tilapia and 1 cup lime juice in a medium glass or stainless steel bowl. Cover with plastic wrap and refrigerate to marinate for about 2 hours or until the fish is opaque and completely "cooked" all the way through. Drain the lime juice off of the fish and add the green onions, bell peppers, cilantro, jalapeño, salt, and remaining 2 tablespoons lime juice. Return to the refrigerator and allow to marinate an additional 30 minutes. Serve with tortilla chips.

Pozole de Calabaza con Carnitas

PORK AND HOMINY SOUP WITH RED CHILES AND PUMPKIN

{ Serves 10 to 12 }

1 2-pound sugar pumpkin or butternut squash (or 2 cups canned unsweetened pumpkin)
2 tablespoons olive oil, divided
1 large ancho chile, stemmed, seeded, deveined and torn into large pieces
1 large guajillo chile, stemmed, seeded, deveined and torn into large pieces
2 cups boiling water
¼ cup water
2 quarts chicken or vegetable stock
1½ pounds pork butt, cut into 1-inch cubes
1 cup diced onion
1 clove of garlic, finely chopped
1 teaspoon dried oregano
2 cups canned hominy, rinsed and drained
Kosher salt and freshly ground pepper
2 cups shredded green cabbage, for garnish
3 radishes, halved and thinly sliced, for garnish
¼ cup diced red onion, for garnish
1 lime cut into wedges, for garnish
Tortilla chips, for serving

~

Preheat oven to 350°. Halve pumpkin or butternut squash, remove seeds and brush with 1 table-spoon of the olive oil. Place cut side down on a rimmed baking sheet and cook until the flesh is soft, 35-45 minutes. Remove to a rack to cool. Once cooled, using a large spoon, remove the flesh to a bowl; set aside.

In a dry 10-inch heavy-bottom sauté pan over medium heat toast the ancho and guajillo chiles until fragrant, for 1-2 minutes. Transfer the toasted chiles to a small bowl and cover with boiling water. Place a slightly smaller heatproof bowl on top to keep the chiles submerged; soak for 30 minutes. After the 30 minutes, drain the chiles, discarding the soaking liquid, and place into a blender with ¼ cup water. Purée until smooth; set aside.

Heat the stock in a large saucepan over medium heat to simmering; do not boil. Heat 1 table-spoon olive oil in a large 8-quart pot over medium-high heat. Once the oil begins to shimmer add the pork and brown on all sides, 8-10 minutes. Add the onion and garlic and cook until fra-grant about 2 minutes. Add the chile puree and oregano and cook for 1-2 minutes more, or until the chile puree begins to darken. Add the warmed stock and stir to combine. Reduce the heat to simmer and cook for 30 minutes. After 30 minutes, add the reserved squash and hominy; simmer an additional 20 minutes or until the pork is tender. Taste and adjust for seasoning with salt and pepper. To serve divide between warm soup bowls. Garnish with cabbage, radishes, onions, limes and tortilla chips; serve immediately.

Pescado al Mojo de Cilantro

GARLIC FISH WITH CILANTRO SAUCE

{ Serves 4 }

1 cup olive oil, divided
½ cup (1 stick) unsalted butter
½ cup peeled garlic cloves
4 6- to 8-ounce skin on pieces of striped bass or any firm fleshed white fish
1 tablespoon sugar
3 teaspoons kosher salt, divided
1 cup apple cider vinegar
1 cup water
1 large red onion, very thinly sliced
3 pickled jalapeños, finely chopped
½ cup pickled jalapeño juice
4 bunches of fresh cilantro, washed and leaves picked from stems, divided
1¼ cups cooked white rice, for serving

~

In a heavy-bottom saucepan over medium heat combine ½ cup of the olive oil, the butter and garlic cloves and bring to a simmer. Reduce heat to low and cook until the garlic begins to turn light brown, 25-30 minutes. Remove the garlic with a slotted spoon and drain on a plate lined with paper towels for later use in the sauce. Transfer the oil and butter mixture to a medium bowl to cool. Once cooled, add the fish, cover with plastic wrap and refrigerate to marinate for at least 2 hours.

Meanwhile, stir together sugar, 1½ teaspoons salt, cider vinegar and water until the salt and sugar are dissolved. Add the sliced onion, making sure the onions are covered in the liquid, and allow to sit for at least 1 hour at room temperature to pickle.

Preheat oven to 200°. In the bowl of a food processor fitted with the blade attachment, combine the jalapeños, jalapeño juice, 3 bunches cilantro leaves, remaining 1½ teaspoons salt, remaining ½ cup of olive oil, and the browned garlic. Process until well combined and somewhat smooth; set aside.

Remove the fish from the refrigerator. In a small saucepan heat the puréed cilantro mixture to a simmer then reduce the heat to low.

Place a wire rack on a rimmed baking sheet and set aside. Preheat the oven to 300°.

Heat a 10-inch non-stick sauté pan over medium-high heat. Add 1 tablespoon of the garlic oil covering the fish, swirl to coat the bottom of the pan. Add 2 pieces of the fish, skin side down, to the pan and cook on each side for 3-4 minutes or until the fish is cooked through. Remove the fish to the prepared baking sheet and place in heated oven to keep warm. Repeat with remaining fish, adding more garlic oil if necessary.

Chop the remaining bunch of cilantro leaves and combine with the cooked rice. To serve, divide the rice between 4 warm plates. Place the fish on top and top with the warm cilantro sauce. Garnish with pickled onions and serve immediately.

Pudin de Pan con Chocolate y Chile

CHOCOLATE CHILE BREAD PUDDING

{ Serves 8 to 10 }

1 tablespoon unsalted butter, for the baking dish
4 ancho chiles, stemmed, seeded and deveined
1 cup brown sugar, firmly packed
⅓ cup warm water
6 large eggs
1 cup granulated sugar
1 teaspoon fine salt
1 cup cocoa powder
1½ cups whole milk
1½ cups heavy cream
2 tablespoons pure vanilla extract
1½ pound loaf of brioche or challah bread cut into ½-inch cubes (about 8 lightly packed cups)
12 ounces white chocolate chips
Ice cream, for serving

~

Preheat oven to 325°. Grease a 13- x 9-inch baking dish with butter and set aside. Place the chiles on a rimmed baking sheet and toast until fragrant, 6-8 minutes. Remove to a rack to cool. Once cool, transfer to a blender or spice grinder and grind into a fine powder.

Combine the brown sugar and water in a small bowl; set aside. Whisk the eggs, granulated sugar and salt together in a medium bowl. Add the cocoa powder and reserved chili powder and mix to combine. Add the brown sugar mixture, milk, cream and vanilla extract and whisk to combine. Combine the bread cubes and white chocolate chips in a very large bowl. Pour the egg mixture over the bread mixture and allow to sit for 25-30 minutes stirring occasionally so that the bread becomes completely saturated. Pour the bread mixture into the prepared baking dish. Bake uncovered for 30 minutes. After 30 minutes, remove the baking dish from the oven, cover with aluminum foil and bake for an additional 35-45 minutes, or until set. Remove to a rack to cool for at least 20 minutes before serving. To serve, cut into squares or triangles and serve immediately with ice cream.

WHAT TO DRINK

While Mexican beers such as Modelo Especial, Corona and XX would be suitable companions to these Mexican delectables, a special margarita brings an extra level of celebration to the equation. Passion fruit adds an exotic twist to this new American staple.

ANTHONY SANDERS

always said he'd become an executive chef before he was 30 and he did. As executive chef at
Sala ~ Sabor de Mexico, he brings his own flair and love for cooking to each dish.
Full of culinary zest and pizzazz, this Apalachicola, Florida native has been
privy to the culinary arts since he was a little boy.

If you could cook a meal for anyone, who would it be?
I'd cook for my mom because she's where I get my values from.

Where would you like to visit that you've never been before?
Europe. I'd like to backpack through the entire continent to see it and taste the food.

Do you speak any foreign languages?
I can say "hot pan" in three different languages.

Most favorite dish to prepare?
Anything with pork.

What are your hobbies?
Basketball, motorcycles, I'm big on motocross.

What's your favorite place to eat when you're not at your own restaurant?
Sol Kitchen in Delray Beach, FL.

If you could have a theme song playing every time you walk into the kitchen, what would it be?
It'd be the theme from *Shaft*.

Who are some famous people you've cooked for?
Serena Williams, Justin Timberlake, Cameron Diaz, and Burt Reynolds.

What food do you find most difficult to work with?
A spice, marjoram. It's too perfumey.

What's your favorite drink?
Armagnac or Cognac.

KEVIN RATHBUN

RATHBUN'S

Greek Easter

Pan Sautéed Kefalatori Cheese

Roasted Organic Beets with Skordalia

Pork and Lamb Keftaides with Tzatziki and Smoked Tomato Puree

Oregano Roasted Lamb Loin with Tomatoes, Feta,
Cucumbers and Greek Olives

Olive Oil Ice Cream with Figs and Greek Honey

Pan Sautéed Kefalatori Cheese

{ Serves 4 }

⅓ cup olive oil
¼ cup buttermilk
1 large egg, lightly beaten
¼ cup all-purpose flour
4 pieces 4- x 3- x ½-inch kefalatori cheese
1 tablespoon freshly squeezed lemon juice
1 tablespoon extra virgin olive oil
1 teaspoon finely grated lemon zest
1 tablespoon finely chopped flat leaf parsley
8 pitted cerignolia olives

~

Heat a non-stick, 9-inch sauté pan over medium heat. Add the olive oil and heat through. Mix buttermilk and egg together in a shallow bowl. Place the flour in a separate shallow bowl. Dip cheese into buttermilk mixture then dredge in the flour. Shake off excess flour and place in the hot oil. Fry the cheese until golden brown, about 3 minutes, turn and brown on the other side. Remove to small serving plates, drizzle with lemon juice and extra virgin olive oil and sprinkle with lemon zest and parsley. Garnish with olives and serve immediately.

"I have custom-made work tables for my restaurant kitchen to accommodate my height. Low tables are not my friends."

Roasted Organic Beets with Skordalia

{ Serves 4 }

1 pound medium-sized organic red beets, stems and roots trimmed
Kosher salt and freshly ground pepper
2 tablespoons olive oil
2 Russet potatoes, scrubbed
⅓ cup heavy cream (warm)
3 slices white bread, crust removed
2 tablespoons minced fresh garlic
¼ cup extra virgin olive oil
2 tablespoons white vinegar
Micro herbs for garnish (oregano, parsley or mint)

~

Place beets in a 2-quart saucepan and add enough water to cover. Add 1 tablespoon salt and bring to a boil. Reduce heat to a low boil and cook beets until fork tender, about 35 minutes. When the beets are done, drain in a colander. Toss with olive oil, season with salt and pepper and rest until cool enough to handle. Rub a little olive oil on your hands and, with a paring knife, peel the beet skins off. Cut the beets in quarters and refrigerate.

Place the potatoes in a saucepan, cover with water, add 1 tablespoon salt and bring to a boil. Reduce heat and simmer until tender, about 20 minutes. Combine the warm cream and bread in a large bowl and mash until smooth. Add garlic, olive oil, vinegar, salt and pepper and mix to combine. Drain, peel and process the potatoes through a ricer or food mill into the bread mixture and stir to combine. Taste and adjust seasoning as needed. Cover and refrigerate.

To serve, divide the potatoes equally between 4 serving plates. Place a spoon of the beets on top of the potatoes and garnish with micro herbs.

Pork and Lamb Keftaides with Tzatziki and Smoked Tomato Puree

{ Serves 4 }

1 pound ground lamb or pork, or a mixture of both
1 tablespoon plus 2 teaspoons finely minced garlic, divided
1 tablespoon finely minced shallot
2 tablespoons plus 2 teaspoons finely chopped mint, divided
1 tablespoon finely chopped parsley
¾ cup heavy cream
¾ cup unseasoned breadcrumbs
2 large eggs, lightly beaten
1 teaspoon salt
½ teaspoon freshly ground pepper
8 ounces Greek yogurt
½ cup seeded and minced cucumbers
1 tablespoon red wine vinegar
2 tablespoons extra virgin olive oil
1 cup hickory wood chips, soaked
2 vine ripe tomatoes, halved

~

In a large bowl, mix ground meat, 1 tablespoon garlic, shallots, 2 tablespoons mint, parsley, heavy cream, breadcrumbs, eggs, 1 teaspoon salt and ½ teaspoon pepper.

Preheat oven to 375°. Line a rimmed baking sheet with parchment paper or a non-stick baking mat (Silpat). Roll meat mixture into 1-ounce meatballs and place on prepared baking sheet. Bake for 10 minutes or until cooked through, depending on size of meatballs.

In a small mixing bowl combine yogurt, cucumbers, remaining 2 teaspoons garlic, remaining 2 teaspoons mint, vinegar, olive oil, salt and pepper. Cover and refrigerate.

Place soaked wood chips in a stove top smoker and turn on. Place tomatoes, cut side up, in the smoker and smoke for 20 minutes. Transfer smoked tomatoes to a blender and blend until smooth. Season with salt and pepper.

Divide meatballs between serving plates. Serve with tzatziki and smoked tomato puree.

"If I could cook a meal for anyone, it would be Harry S. Truman. I think it would be quite educational. I'm not even sure what I'd ask him."

Oregano Roasted Lamb Loin
with Tomatoes, Feta, Cucumbers and Greek Olives

{ Serves 6 }

2 Colorado lamb racks
3 teaspoons kosher salt, divided
1½ teaspoons freshly ground pepper, divided
1 tablespoon minced garlic
1 tablespoon dried oregano
1 tablespoon finely chopped fresh flat leaf parsley
¼ cup extra virgin olive oil
2 tablespoons red wine vinegar
1 teaspoon freshly squeezed lemon juice
1 tablespoon finely minced shallots
2 cored and medium-diced vine ripe tomatoes
1½ cups medium-diced peeled cucumber
4 ounces feta cheese, cut into ½-inch cubes
16 Greek olives
2 tablespoons olive oil
¼ cup micro basil

~

Remove rack bones from loins and discard. Season loins with 2 teaspoons salt, 1 teaspoon pepper and rub with garlic, oregano and parsley. Set aside.

In a small bowl whisk together extra virgin olive oil, vinegar, lemon juice, shallots, remaining teaspoon salt and ½ teaspoon pepper; let stand at room temperature until serving time.

In a medium bowl, gently toss tomatoes, cucumber, feta and olives just until combined.

Preheat oven to 400°. Heat a heavy-bottom, oven-proof sauté pan over high heat. Add olive oil and swirl to coat bottom of pan. Add the lamb loins and sauté, turning after 2 minutes, until golden brown on all sides. Transfer the sauté pan to the preheated oven and continue to cook until rare or internal temperature reaches 130° about 8-10 minutes, depending on size of loin. Transfer to a cutting board and let rest 3 minutes.

To serve, divide the tomato salad equally between 6 plates. Slice the loin, divide between the plates, drizzle with vinaigrette and garnish with micro basil.

Olive Oil Ice Cream with Figs and Greek Honey

{ Serves 6 }

6 large egg yolks
¾ cup granulated sugar
1 cup heavy cream
2 cups half and half
1 vanilla bean
½ cup extra virgin olive oil
1 pint fresh Mission figs
⅓ cup Greek honey
Fresh mint leaves
Confectioners' sugar

In a large bowl, whisk the yolks and sugar until light and frothy.

Combine the cream and half and half in a heavy-bottom saucepan. Split the vanilla bean lengthwise and, with the tip of a paring knife, scrape the inside of the bean to remove the seeds. Add the seeds and scraped pod to the cream mixture and bring to a boil, stirring occasionally to prevent scorching. Remove from heat. Add a little of the hot cream mixture into the egg yolk mixture to temper. Slowly mix the remaining cream into the yolk mixture and stir. Pour the mixture back into the saucepan and cook on medium heat, stirring continuously, until the custard is slightly thick and coats the back of a spoon, about 5 minutes. If the mixture starts to boil or curdle, remove from the heat, continue stirring to cool and reduce the heat to low and continue to cook. Strain the custard through a fine mesh sieve into a glass or stainless bowl. Whisking constantly, slowly drizzle the olive oil into the warm custard and chill. For a quick chill, place the bowl in an ice bath and whisk to quickly cool. Freeze the chilled custard in an ice cream freezer according to the manufacturer's instructions. Pack the ice cream into an airtight container and freeze for 2-3 hours or until firm.

To serve, split figs in half lengthwise. Place a generous scoop of ice cream in center of fig and sandwich together. Drizzle with Greek honey and garnish with mint and confectioners' sugar.

WHAT TO DRINK

When talk turns to Greek wines, thoughts go to retsina, Greece's pine-laden white classic, but there are many other wines from which to choose. For a great intro to Greek reds, select one made from St. George or as they're called in Greece, the agiorghitiko grape. Luscious cherry flavors are buffered by mineral character and mature tannins. The wines are literally made for lamb.

KEVIN RATHBUN

started cooking when he was 14 and by 17 knew he wanted to be a chef. His mom and dad were the greatest influences on his career. His dad's advice helped guide him through life. His mom was a maitre d' at a fine restaurant, and she wore a tux at work and knew how to handle guests. "My tableside manner came from watching her."

What's your favorite drink?
Gin and tonic with Hendrick's gin or Boodles. The first drink I ever had was Beefeater gin on the rocks when I was mighty young.

What's your favorite time of day?
Cool mornings. It's comfortable. It's the beginning of a brand new day.

What was the first dish you learned to cook?
Smoked brisket. I learned how to cook it and learned how to barbecue from my dad. I'll cook a brisket for 18-20 hours before serving it.

What would you do if you won the lottery?
I'd build different restaurants with different concepts. But, I wouldn't stop working. I don't think I'll ever stop working.

What's your most used quote in the kitchen?
"It needs more salt!"

Where do you eat on your day off?
Houston's. It's my wife's favorite restaurant.

If you could have another job for a day, what would it be?
I'd be a restaurant designer. I find it fun to be able to create.

What are the words you live by?
Respect and passion.

What's your favorite guilty pleasure?
Cigars.

145

JUSTIN KEITH

Champagne and Celebration
—

Chilled Lobster Shots with Coconut-Tarragon Vinaigrette
Serrano Ham and Manchego Croque Monsieur
Honey Glazed Shrimp with Chipotle-Louis Dressing
German Lamb Sausage with Spicy Grain Mustard
Boursin Stuffed Strawberries with Thyme-Balsamic Reduction

Chilled Lobster Shots with Coconut-Tarragon Vinaigrette

{ Serves 4 }

1 fresh bay leaf
1 cup chopped onion (1 medium)
½ cup chopped carrot (about 2 small carrots)
½ cup chopped celery (about 2 stalks)
2 lemons, halved plus 1 lemon wedge for garnish
1 large lobster tail, (10 to 12 ounces) shell on
½ cup unsweetened coconut milk
¼ cup sour cream
1 teaspoon fresh chopped tarragon
1 tablespoon champagne vinegar
2 dashes Tabasco
¼ cup toasted grated coconut, for garnish
Kosher salt and freshly ground pepper

~

Fill a 2½-quart saucepan three-fourths full with water. Add the bay leaf, onion, carrot, celery, and lemon halves. Bring to a boil then reduce the heat to simmer. Cook until fragrant and flavorful, about 15 minutes. Increase the temperature to boil. Add the lobster tail and boil on high for 90 seconds; turn heat off, cover and let sit for 8 minutes. Remove lobster tail to a paper towel lined plate and refrigerate until chilled, about 1 hour.

Using kitchen shears cut the underside membrane of the lobster tail. Split the shell to expose and remove the tail meat. Remove the vein and rinse to wash away any remaining shell or grit. Dice the tail meat, transfer to a small bowl and set aside.

For the dressing, in small mixing bowl combine the coconut milk, sour cream, chopped tarragon, vinegar, and Tabasco. Season with salt and pepper.

Add just enough dressing to coat the lobster. Return to refrigerator for 30 minutes to chill.

Moisten the rims of 4 shot glasses with the lemon wedge. Place the toasted coconut on a shallow plate and rim the edges of the shot glasses in the toasted coconut.

Taste the lobster mixture and adjust for seasoning with salt and pepper. Spoon the lobster mixture into the prepared shot glasses. Pass them around and make a toast!

"In the winter I love to make chili and during the summer I love to experiment with barbeque . . . especially trying new dry rubs and sauces."

Serrano Ham and Manchego Croque Monsieur

{ Serves 4 to 6 }

10 slices brioche or white bread
10 slices of Serrano ham (prosciutto or country ham could be substituted)
½ pound Manchego cheese, thinly sliced
3 large eggs, lightly beaten
¼ cup half and half
Pinch of kosher salt
Pinch of freshly ground pepper
2 tablespoons unsalted butter
Fig Jam Dipping Sauce

~

Using a large biscuit cutter, cut the centers out of the bread. Discard the crusts or reserve for another use. Place 5 of the bread rounds on the counter and layer each round with ham and cheese and top with the remaining 5 rounds.

In a medium bowl, beat eggs, half and half, salt and pepper until well combined. Heat a large skillet over medium heat. Add the butter and heat until sizzling. Carefully dip each sandwich in egg mixture to coat, then place in the hot skillet. Working in batches, brown on both sides until the cheese is melted. To serve, place the sandwiches on a warm platter and serve with fig jam dipping sauce.

FIG JAM DIPPING SAUCE

1 cup prepared fig jam
½ cup pomegranate juice
1 cinnamon stick

~

Combine the fig jam, pomegranate juice and cinnamon stick in a small saucepan over medium heat. Simmer until the jam has dissolved and the mixture is well combined, 10-12 minutes. Reduce heat to low and hold warm, stirring occasionally.

Honey Glazed Shrimp with Chipotle-Louis Dressing

{ Serves 4 }

1 cup mayonnaise
1 chipotle pepper in adobe sauce (canned)
1 tablespoon finely chopped fresh flat leaf parsley
¼ cup lemon juice
1 tablespoon plus ½ teaspoon finely grated fresh horseradish
¼ cup finely diced onion
2 tablespoons cider vinegar
1 dash Tabasco
Kosher salt and freshly ground pepper
2 tablespoons canola oil
12 large shrimp, peeled and deveined
1 teaspoon chopped garlic
¼ cup honey
¼ cup wheat beer
2 tablespoons unsalted butter

~

For the dressing: In the bowl of a food processor fitted with the blade attachment combine the mayonnaise, chipotle, parsley, lemon juice, horseradish, onion, vinegar, and Tabasco. Season with salt and pepper; purée until combined. Transfer dressing to a small bowl; set aside.

Heat the oil in large skillet on medium-high heat until shimmering. Pat the shrimp with a paper towel to remove any excess water; season both sides with salt and pepper. Add to hot skillet and cook until curled and pink, about 2 minutes per side. Add the garlic, honey, and beer. Continue to cook until the honey starts to caramelize, an additional 2 minutes. Remove from the heat. Add the butter and stir to combine. Taste and adjust for seasoning with salt and pepper. Immediately remove the shrimp to a platter. Serve with the reserved dressing on the side. Season with salt and pepper and serve chilled.

German Lamb Sausage with Spicy Grain Mustard

{ Makes 30 }

1 teaspoon canola oil for brushing baking sheet
1½ pounds ground lamb
½ cup breadcrumbs
½ cup finely diced onion
½ cup finely diced sun-dried tomatoes
¼ cup finely diced poblano pepper
¼ cup Jägermeister
3 large eggs, room temperature, lightly beaten
1 tablespoon finely chopped oregano
2 teaspoons finely chopped garlic
1¼ teaspoons cumin
1 teaspoon fennel seed
1 teaspoon kosher salt
1 teaspoon freshly ground pepper
Favorite mustard, for dipping (whole grain, spicy, Dijon, etc.)
Sliced green onions, for garnish

~

Heat the oven to 375°. Brush a rimmed baking sheet with oil; set aside. Combine the lamb, breadcrumbs, onion, tomatoes, pepper, Jägermeister, eggs, oregano, garlic, cumin, fennel seed, salt and pepper in a large bowl.

Using a small ice cream scoop or tablespoon, form quarter sized meatballs with the lamb mixture. Place meatballs 2 inches apart on the prepared baking sheet. Transfer to the oven and bake until cooked through, about 15 minutes. Remove from the oven to cool slightly. Serve with toothpicks, mustard, and green onions for garnish.

Boursin Stuffed Strawberries with Thyme-Balsamic Reduction

{ Serves 4 }

1½ cups balsamic vinegar
2 sprigs fresh thyme
½ cup honey
8 medium–large fresh strawberries
½ cup Boursin Garlic & Fine Herbs cheese
½ cup cream cheese
Kosher salt and freshly ground pepper

~

Pour balsamic vinegar and honey into a small saucepan and add thyme. Bring almost to a boil on medium-high heat and then reduce heat to low. Simmer until reduced by two-thirds or until syrup consistency, about 30 minutes. Remove from heat, remove and discard the thyme sprigs. Cool the balsamic reduction to room temperature. The mixture will thicken as it cools.

In a stand mixer with paddle attachment, whip the Boursin and cream cheese until doubled in size and soft enough to spread. Season with a pinch of salt and pepper.

Remove stems from strawberries and slice in half, lengthwise. Use a small melon ball scoop to remove some of the interior of the berries and discard.

Spoon or pipe the cheese mixture in to the strawberries and place on a platter. If a berry will not remain upright, slice off a small section of the bottom so it is flat. Drizzle a small amount of cooled balsamic reduction across the tops of the berries and serve.

WHAT TO DRINK

There's more to sparkling wine than just Champagne. Although they cannot carry the legendary moniker of France's prestigious sparkler, top quality sparkling wines hail from all over the globe. Here are a couple to look out for:

CAVA Produced primarily in Catalonia outside of Barçelona, these wines tend to be lighter, more refreshing than Champagne. The grapes used are macabeo, xarello and parellada.

PROSECCO Italy's sparkling treat made from the grape of the same name. The wines vary from bone dry to semi-sweet. The wine serves as the versatile base to the now regal Bellini from Venice.

JUSTIN KEITH

thought he wanted to be an FBI agent when he was young, but looking back he says food has been in his blood from the beginning. Being raised as one of three children by a single mom, everyone had to help out. "If you helped with dinner you didn't have to do dishes. That was enough to get me in the kitchen." Growing up, Justin remembers spending weekends on his grandparents' farm in South Georgia. "We'd spend all weekend picking, cleaning and putting up corn, fruits and other vegetables for winter. It was hard work but somehow I always enjoyed it."

What's your favorite guilty pleasure?
Once or twice a month, really late at night I love picking up a few Krystal cheeseburgers.

What's your favorite kitchen tool?
My Microplane grater.

What foods do you find most difficult to work with?
Desserts.

If you could have another job for a day, what would it be?
A musician for a rock or bluegrass band. I don't play any instruments, but other than that I'm pretty musical.

What's your favorite place to eat when you're not at your restaurant?
For casual dining I love Nuevo Laredo and Dreamland BBQ. For fine dining, Rathbun's and Aria.

Where would you like to visit that you've never been before?
Fiji.

What people have been the most inspirational to you and your career?
My mom has always been a huge supporter and a motivator for me. Professionally, I think probably Thomas Keller.

LINDA HARRELL

MEEHAN'S PUBLIC HOUSE

Luck of the Irish

—

Guinness Battered Fish and Chips

Tipperary Cheddar and Herb Irish Soda Bread

Maple–Jalapeño Irish Bacon

Napa Valley Champ Potatoes

Bailey's Panna Cotta with Fresh Rhubarb Sauce

Guinness Battered Fish and Chips

{ Serves 4 }

3 cups all-purpose flour
½ cup cornstarch
1 teaspoon garlic powder
½ teaspoon black pepper
½ teaspoon iodized salt
4 4-ounce pieces fresh white fish filets (cod or haddock)
1 bottle of Guinness Stout, chilled, additional for drinking
Canola oil for frying
Chips
Malt vinegar for serving
Tartar Sauce

~

In a small mixing bowl, blend the flour, cornstarch, garlic powder, pepper and salt together. Pour the Guinness in a second small bowl. Fill a mini home fryer or a large Dutch oven half full with oil. Heat oil to 350°. Test to see if it's hot enough by taking a pinch of flour and flicking into the oil. If it dissipates rapidly, the oil is ready.

Place a cooling rack on a rimmed baking sheet and set aside.

Dip a fish filet into the Guinness, then dredge in the flour, shaking off excess. Dip back in the Guinness and then back in the flour. Carefully place each battered piece into the hot oil. When the fish is a golden brown and floating, remove with a skimmer (spider) or slotted spoon to the prepared baking sheet. Place the cooked fish in a 300° oven or warming drawer to keep warm. Reserve the hot oil for the chips.

To serve, portion the fish and chips between 4 plates. Serve with malt vinegar and tartar sauce. Pour a glass of Guinness stout and enjoy.

"I'm proud of how far I've come in my career. When I started out girls didn't become chefs; when I earned my first chef position at age 19 I felt I had made a huge achievement."

CHIPS

2 pounds Russet potatoes cut into ¼- x 4-inch batons
Kosher salt and freshly ground pepper

~

Return the oil to 350°. Add the potatoes. Cook until golden and crisp, about 4 minutes. Remove from oil and place on a paper towel lined plate to drain. Season immediately with salt and pepper. (The reason for cooking the fries after the fish is that the potatoes release a large amount of water into the oil. The water will break the oil down and make it difficult to get the crisp crunchy texture for the fish.)

TARTAR SAUCE

2 cups mayonnaise
2 tablespoons finely minced onion
1 tablespoon finely chopped parsley
2 tablespoons finely chopped cornichons (crisp, tart tiny gherkin cucumber pickles)
¼ cup red wine vinegar
1 tablespoon finely minced scallion
2 tablespoons capers, drained
1 dash Worcestershire
2 dashes Tabasco
Kosher salt and freshly ground pepper

~

In a small mixing bowl, stir together the mayonnaise, onion, parsley, cornichons, vinegar, scallion, capers and season to taste with Worcestershire, Tabasco, salt and pepper.

Tipperary Cheddar and Herb Irish Soda Bread

{ Makes 2 small loaves }

4 cups all-purpose flour, additional for board
1 teaspoon baking soda
1 teaspoon cream of tartar
1 teaspoon salt
3 tablespoons sugar
1 tablespoon finely chopped fresh oregano
1 tablespoon finely chopped fresh thyme
2 tablespoons finely chopped scallion
½ cup Tipperary cheddar (or a nice aged Vermont cheddar)
2 cups buttermilk

~

Preheat oven to 375°. In a large mixing bowl, whisk the flour, baking soda, cream of tartar, salt and sugar to combine. Add the oregano, thyme, scallion and cheese. Create a well in the middle of the flour mixture and, using a fork, stir in the buttermilk. Stir briskly until the dough holds together in a rough mass.

Turn the dough out onto a lightly floured surface. Knead gently for about 30 seconds. Divide dough in half and form each half into a small loaf. Dust lightly with flour and place onto a parchment or silicone baking mat lined rimmed baking sheet. Place in preheated oven and bake for about 30-35 minutes, until golden. The loaves should sound a bit hollow when you tap them. Transfer to a rack to cool. Cool completely before serving.

With an Irish mother and immediate family still in Belfast, Harrell enjoys taking traditional dishes and making them new and fresh for today's tastes.

Maple–Jalapeño Irish Bacon

{ Makes 2 pounds }

8 cups water
½ cup kosher salt
½ cup pure maple syrup
¼ cup brown sugar
½ cup finely diced yellow onion
2 sliced fresh jalapeño peppers
2 tablespoons finely chopped fresh oregano
1 tablespoon whole black peppercorns
2 pounds boneless pork loin

~

Combine the water, salt, syrup, sugar, onion, jalapeños, oregano and peppercorns in a large saucepan. Bring the mixture to a boil and stir to dissolve the sugar. Remove from the heat and set aside to let cool to room temperature. To hasten the cooling, you may stir in a few ice cubes.

When the brine has cooled, place the pork in brine and refrigerate for 8 hours, or overnight. Remove the pork and discard the brine. With the pork still very cold, cut the cured "bacon" into slices about ¼-inch thick.

To serve, cook slices in a skillet or on a griddle until pink or medium. If you have any raw pork left over, refrigerate and use within 3 days or freeze.

Napa Valley Champ Potatoes

{ Serves 6 }

2 pounds Yukon gold potatoes
5 tablespoons unsalted butter
½ cup diced Maple-Jalapeño Bacon
½ cup finely chopped green onions
1½ cups diced Napa cabbage (about ½ small head)
1 cup whole milk
Kosher salt and freshly ground pepper

Peel potatoes, cut into quarters and place in a large Dutch oven; add water to cover. Bring to a boil and cook until fork tender, about 25 minutes. Remove from the heat and drain in a colander. Place drained potatoes back in the hot pan to evaporate any water and until the potatoes are completely dry. Remove the potatoes back to the colander and set aside.

Add the butter to the Dutch oven and heat over medium heat until melted. Add the diced bacon and cook until the fat is rendered and the bacon is light pink in color, about 8 minutes. Adjust the temperature so the bacon doesn't brown and crisp, but stays soft. Increase the temperature to medium-high; add the green onions and sauté for 2 minutes. Add the cabbage and continue to sauté until tender, about 5 minutes. Add the milk and bring to a simmer. When the mixture comes to a simmer, add the cooked potatoes back to the pan. Mash potatoes into the mixture with a potato masher to break up and finish with a wooden spoon until all ingredients are mixed together. Season the potatoes with salt and pepper and serve.

(One of my favorite ways to eat this is when it's finished, put the mixture into a piping hot sauté pan and fry it, almost like a farl. Like Mom used to make, except better.)

Bailey's Panna Cotta with Fresh Rhubarb Sauce

{ Serves 4 }

1½ teaspoons (1 envelope) unflavored gelatin
2 cups heavy whipping cream, divided
½ cup sugar
½ cup Bailey's Irish Cream
1 tablespoon butter for plastic wrap
Fresh Rhubarb Sauce
Strawberries for garnish

~

In a small bowl, soften the gelatin in 3 tablespoons cream. Set aside for 5 minutes. In a saucepan, heat the remaining cream and sugar over medium-high heat, stirring occasionally. When the sugar has dissolved, whisk ¼ cup of the hot mixture into the softened gelatin and stir. Slowly stir the dissolved gelatin mixture in to the hot cream until the gelatin has dissolved. Remove from the heat and stir in Bailey's and mix well. Pour in to individual ramekins or stemmed glasses, filling three-fourths full, leaving space to later add the sauce. Cover the ramekins with buttered plastic wrap to prevent skin from forming. Refrigerate until firm.

To serve, spoon rhubarb sauce over panna cotta. Garnish with fresh strawberries. When in season, lemon verbena is a wonderful garnish for this dish.

FRESH RHUBARB SAUCE

1 pound diced fresh rhubarb
½ pint fresh strawberries, stemmed and quartered
3 tablespoons frozen orange juice concentrate (⅓ small can)
½ teaspoon ground cinnamon
⅓ cup granulated sugar
⅓ cup water
½ vanilla bean

~

Place rhubarb, strawberries, orange juice concentrate, cinnamon, sugar and water in a saucepan over low heat. Split the vanilla bean lengthwise and scrape the seeds out with the tip of a knife. Add the vanilla bean seeds to the sauce and let simmer slowly until rhubarb and strawberries are tender, about 10 minutes. Remove from the heat. Cool slightly. In a blender, or using immersion blender, purée the mixture until smooth.

WHAT TO DRINK

What better way to celebrate the luck of the Irish than with a refreshing Irish ale? The only problem is to decide whether Guinness' creamy, dark stout is what strikes your fancy or Harp's crisp, hoppiness is what you crave. Why decide? With a black and tan, the best of both worlds converge to provide the richness of Guinness and the refreshing nature of Harp.

HERE'S WHAT YOU NEED
Traditional pint glasses
Supply of Guinness Stout
Supply of Harp Ale
Upside-down bent spoon that fits midway down the pint glass

HERE'S WHAT YOU DO
Fill the glass halfway with Harp, taking care to produce a
    hearty head.
Place the spoon midway down the glass with the tip touching
    the side and just breaking the surface of the Harp.
Pour the Guinness slow and steady over the spoon.
Serve immediately.

LINDA HARRELL

fell in love with the kitchen during her first job in a Baltimore restaurant at age 13. She had to stand on a crate just to core lettuce heads and peel garlic. She eventually went on to study English at the College of William and Mary in Virginia before channeling her creativity into cooking. "Looking back, the signs were always there. I loved being in the kitchen as a kid. I tried to make my dad goulash once and I ruined it by adding way too much paprika. I didn't think it looked right without it. Even then I was altering recipes."

Where would you like to visit that you've never been before?
Pitcairn Island. It has such a cool story and I hear it is beautiful.

If you could cook a meal for anyone, who would it be?
I'd love the chance to cook for my grandmother before she died.

What is your favorite guilty pleasure?
I absolutely love Neal Boortz's radio show.

If you could have a theme song playing every time you walk into the kitchen, what would it be?
"Ain't No Mountain High Enough" by Marvin Gaye and Tammi Terrell.

What is your favorite dish to prepare?
I love to cook any dish, but I'm always most excited about a great new creation.

Do you have a favorite book or author?
Any poetry by Dylan Thomas and any novel by James Michener.

What were your meals at home like when you were growing up?
They were great because my mother cooked lots of unusual vegetables like rutabaga, Brussels sprouts and cauliflower. I still love all those vegetables and so many people never even try them.

MARK ALBA

THE FOOD STUDIO

Dinner Party to Impress

Roasted Corn Soup with Smoked Bacon Flan

Butter Poached Lobster Salad with Champagne-Caviar Vinaigrette

Halibut with Fingerling Potatoes,
Cabbage, English Peas and Truffle Cream

Roasted Rack of Lamb with Celery Root Puree
and Red Onion Marmalade

Cherry Cobbler with Vanilla Bean Ice Cream

Roasted Corn Soup with Smoked Bacon Flan

{ Serves 8 }

6 ears fresh corn, in the husk
2 tablespoons unsalted butter
1 tablespoon olive oil
1 cup diced onion (1 medium onion)
⅓ cup chopped celery (2 stalks)
1 teaspoon chopped garlic
1 cup heavy cream
Kosher salt and freshly ground pepper
Bacon Flan

~

Heat oven to 350°. Roast the corn in the husk for 25 minutes. Remove from the oven and carefully remove the husks and silks. Scrape the kernels from each ear of corn and set aside for later use. Place the scraped corn cobs in a large saucepan and cover with 6 cups water. Bring corn cobs to a boil, reduce heat and simmer for 1 hour.

Heat a large saucepan over medium-high heat. Add the butter and oil and heat until the butter is melted. Add the onion, celery and garlic and cook until soft, about 5 minutes. Reduce the heat to medium, add the corn, and cook for 5 minutes. Strain the corn cob stock into the vegetables and bring to a boil. Reduce the heat and simmer, uncovered for 20 minutes. Add the cream and continue simmer for another 5 minutes.

Ladle the soup into a blender, and purée until smooth. Work in batches as needed. Strain the soup through a chinois or other fine mesh strainer. Return the strained soup to the pan and keep warm. Season to taste with salt and pepper.

To serve, un-mold flans into center of shallow soup plate and ladle about 6 ounces of soup over the flan.

"Basil is a lab-chow mix. I don't go anywhere without him, though it would be hard to have him running around the kitchen!"

BACON FLAN

2 tablespoons unsalted butter, for ramekins
8 ounces applewood smoked bacon
3 large eggs
1½ cups heavy cream
Kosher salt and freshly ground pepper

~

Preheat oven to 275°.

Rub the inside of 4 small ramekins with butter and set aside.

Heat a large skillet over medium heat. Add the bacon and cook until browned and crisp, turning once after about 3 minutes. Drain the cooked bacon on a paper towel lined plate. Reserve the bacon fat.

In a saucepan, bring 2 cups of water to a boil. Set aside.

Combine the eggs, cream, bacon and 2 tablespoons bacon fat in the container of a blender and allow the mixture to sit for five minutes. Purée the mixture until smooth. Strain through a chinois or other fine mesh strainer into a pitcher. Season with salt and pepper.

Divide the mixture between 6 ramekins. Place the ramekins on rimmed baking sheet and place in oven. Add enough boiling water to the baking sheet to cover the bottom of the pan. Bake 20-30 minutes or until the top is just set. Carefully remove the pan from the oven, being careful not to spill the hot water. Remove the flans from the pan to a cooling rack and allow to cool and set about 10 minutes before serving.

Butter Poached Lobster Salad
with Champagne-Caviar Vinaigrette

{ Serves 4 }

2 live lobsters, 1–1½ pounds each
1 pound unsalted butter, cut into ½-inch cubes
4 small shallots, divided
1½ teaspoons minced garlic
1 bay leaf
1 teaspoon whole black peppercorns
2 tablespoons fresh lemon juice
1 teaspoon orange zest
2 teaspoons kosher salt
5 sprigs tarragon
2 teaspoons olive oil
½ cup freshly squeezed orange juice
8 ounces champagne
½ teaspoon Dijon mustard
2 tablespoons honey
2 tablespoons champagne vinegar
¼ teaspoon freshly ground pepper
½ cup best quality extra virgin olive oil
1 tablespoon caviar
1 tablespoon tarragon chiffonade
6 ounces mâche, micro-greens or baby spring mix
1 cup grape tomatoes, quartered
1 ripe avocado, diced

~

Fill a large stock pot with water and bring to a boil. Fill a very large bowl with ice and water to make an ice bath. Immerse the lobsters in the boiling water and cook for 3 minutes. Remove the lobsters from the pot and immediately plunge into the ice bath. Once the lobsters are cool enough to handle, remove from the water and place on a towel. Twist the tails off the lobsters and using kitchen shears, cut the shells lengthwise down the underside of the body. Carefully peel the shells from the meat. Remove the vein from the meat and discard. Rinse the tail to remove any remaining shell or vein. Gently crack the claws and remove the meat. Crack and remove the meat from the knuckles. Set the lobster meat aside.

"I'm a huge fan of Jeeps, I've had five Jeeps."

In a 2-quart saucepan over medium heat, bring 2 tablespoons of water to a boil. Slowly whisk in the butter a few pieces at a time until the butter and water are emulsified. Reduce the heat to medium-low, to hold at about 140°, just below a simmer. Add 3 thinly sliced shallots, the garlic, bay leaf, peppercorns, lemon juice, orange zest, kosher salt, and 5 tarragon sprigs. Place the lobster meat in the poaching liquid and cook until the meat is cooked through, about 4-5 minutes.

Remove the lobster with a slotted spoon and drain on a paper towel lined plate. Chill until ready to serve.

Place a small sauté pan over medium heat and add the olive oil. Once the oil is hot, add 1 minced shallot to the pan and cook until translucent, about 1 minute. Add the orange juice to deglaze the pan. Once the juice has almost evaporated, pour in the champagne. Remove from heat and place mixture into medium stainless mixing bowl. Whisk in the mustard, honey, vinegar, and pepper. Continue whisking vigorously while you slowly drizzle in the extra virgin olive oil, forming an emulsion. Gently fold in the caviar and chiffonade of tarragon.

To serve, combine the greens, tomatoes and avocadoes in a large mixing bowl. Drizzle about 6-8 tablespoons of the dressing over the salad, and toss to combine. Chop the reserved lobster meat into bite-sized pieces and add to the salad. Season to taste with salt and pepper. Divide the salad between 4 chilled plates and serve immediately.

Halibut with Fingerling Potatoes, Cabbage, English Peas and Truffle Cream

{ Serves 4 }

1 pound fingerling potatoes, sliced on an angle, ¼-inch thick
½ cup chicken stock
1 small carrot, peeled and diced into ¼-inch cubes
1 cup shelled English peas
1 small head Savoy cabbage (about 1 pound), cored and cut into ¼-inch slices
1 cup heavy cream
3 tablespoons extra virgin olive oil
4 5-ounce halibut filets
1 tablespoon Roasted Garlic Paste
½ teaspoon truffle oil
2 tablespoons unsalted butter
Kosher salt and freshly ground pepper

~

Place the potatoes in a saucepan and add water to cover. Add 2 teaspoons salt and bring to a boil over high heat. Reduce heat to simmer and cook until tender, about 4 minutes. Drain in a colander and set aside. Add the chicken stock to the now empty saucepan and bring to a boil. Add the carrots, they should be covered with stock, if more stock is needed, add a little, just to cover. Cook 3 minutes and add peas (again, adding a little more stock to cover as needed) and cook until tender, about 3 more minutes. Remove the carrots and peas from the stock with a slotted spoon to the colander with the potatoes. Return the stock to a boil and add the cabbage and cook until wilted, about 3 minutes. Add the cream and reduce the heat to low and simmer for about 10 minutes, until the sauce begins to thicken.

Heat a large skillet over medium-high heat. Add the oil and swirl to cover the bottom of the pan. Season the halibut on both sides with salt and pepper. Place the fish in the sauté pan and cook until crisp and golden, about 3 minutes. Turn and cook until golden, about 2-3 minutes. Reduce the heat to medium and cook until the halibut is opaque throughout, an additional 2-3 minutes.

Once the cabbage is cooked and the sauce thickened, stir in the roasted garlic paste, truffle oil and butter. Stir to combine, fold in the reserved vegetables and season to taste with salt and pepper.

To serve, using a slotted spoon, divide the vegetables between 4 warm serving plates. Place the halibut on top of each serving of vegetables and spoon some of the extra sauce around the vegetables and on top of the fish. Serve immediately.

ROASTED GARLIC PASTE

1 whole head garlic
1 tablespoon olive oil
Kosher salt and freshly ground pepper

~

Preheat oven to 350°. Remove any loose papery outer skin of the garlic, leaving the head intact. Cut the top ¼ inch off of the garlic and discard. Place the cut head on an 8-inch square of aluminum foil. Drizzle liberally with olive oil and season with salt and pepper. Wrap tightly and roast in the oven for about an hour or until the garlic is golden brown and tender. Remove from oven, open the foil and allow to cool. Squeeze the soft garlic from the head onto a clean work surface. Mash with a fork to create a paste. Store covered in an airtight container in the refrigerator for up to one week.

Roasted Rack of Lamb with Celery Root Puree and Red Onion Marmalade

{ Serves 4 }

1 medium garlic clove, peeled and roughly chopped
1 medium shallot, peeled and roughly chopped
½ teaspoon black peppercorns
½ teaspoon herbes de Provence
2 teaspoons extra virgin olive oil
1 tablespoon pomegranate molasses
1 rack of lamb, bones Frenched
Kosher salt to taste
Red Onion Marmalade
Celery Root Puree
Pomegranate seeds, for garnish

~

Pulse garlic, shallot, peppercorns, herbes de Provence, olive oil, and pomegranate molasses in a food processor to form a rough paste. Rub paste onto the lamb rack and allow to rest, covered, at room temperature for 1½ hours or in the refrigerator for up to 24 hours.

Preheat grill to medium-high. Wipe the rub from the lamb rack and season with salt. Grill over a hot fire to your desired degree of doneness, 125° for rare. For medium-rare to medium lamb, grill about 5 minutes on each side. Remove from the grill and allow to rest for 5 minutes. Cut the rack into individual chops.

To plate the finished dish, mound some of the celery root puree in the center of plate, lean 2 chops against each other and rest on the celery puree, garnish with a generous spoon of red onion marmalade and a sprinkling of sparkling red pomegranate seeds.

"My fondest childhood memory is of my grandmother making arequipe from scratch. Arequipe takes countless hours of stirring. I remember watching her make this as she watched her Spanish soap operas."

RED ONION MARMALADE

{ Makes ½ cup }

2 tablespoons extra virgin olive oil
2 medium red onions, peeled and sliced ½-inch thick
2 tablespoons balsamic vinegar
1 tablespoon red wine vinegar
Kosher salt and freshly ground pepper to taste

～

Heat a 10-inch heavy sauté pan over medium heat. Add oil and swirl to coat the bottom of the pan. Add onions, 1 teaspoon salt and ½ teaspoon pepper, and cook, stirring frequently, for about 10 minutes, or until the onions begin to soften. Add balsamic and red wine vinegars. Cover the surface of the onions with a disk of parchment paper and cover the pan with a tight fitting lid. Reduce heat to very low and allow to cook, undisturbed, for 1 hour. Season to taste with salt and pepper and keep warm.

CELERY ROOT PUREE

{ Makes 2 cups }

1 celery root, approximately 1½ pounds, peeled and cut into rough chunks
2 cups whole milk
½ teaspoon kosher salt
¼ teaspoon freshly ground pepper
1 tablespoon extra virgin olive oil

～

Combine celery root and milk in a medium saucepan. Bring to a simmer, partially cover, and simmer until fork tender, approximately 30 minutes. Using a slotted spoon, remove celery root from pan and reserve the cooking liquid. Whip the celery root with a stand mixer fitted with the paddle attachment. Stir in the salt, pepper, and olive oil. If necessary, add some of the reserved cooking liquid to adjust the consistency. Keep warm.

Cherry Cobbler with Vanilla Bean Ice Cream

2 14.5-ounce cans pitted tart red cherries
1¼ cups sugar
3 tablespoons cornstarch
1 cup flour
¼ cup sugar
2 tablespoons brown sugar
1 teaspoon baking powder
½ teaspoon cinnamon
4 tablespoons unsalted butter, plus more for baking dish
1 large egg, lightly beaten
3 tablespoons milk
Vanilla Bean Ice Cream

~

Preheat oven to 400°. With a paper towel, rub the inside of a 2-quart baking dish with butter and set aside.

In a large saucepan combine cherries and juice, sugar and cornstarch and stir until mixture is smooth and cornstarch is dissolved. Stir and cook over medium-high heat, until bubbling and thickened, mixture will go from cloudy to clear. Transfer mixture to prepared baking dish.

In a medium bowl, stir flour, sugars, baking powder, and cinnamon to combine. Cut in butter until mixture resembles coarse meal. Stir in the egg and milk with a fork just until combined. Drop topping by tablespoonfuls onto filling. Bake for 25 minutes until browned and bubbly. Serve warm with homemade vanilla ice cream.

VANILLA BEAN ICE CREAM

2½ cups heavy cream
1 cup whole milk
1½ cups sugar
2 vanilla beans
3 large eggs

~

In a heavy-bottom saucepan, combine the cream, milk and sugar. With a knife, cut vanilla beans in half lengthwise. With the tip of a paring knife, scrape the seeds into the cream mixture. Add the pods and bring mixture just to a boil, stirring occasionally to prevent scorching. Remove pan from heat.

In a large bowl, lightly beat the eggs. Add a little of the hot cream mixture to the eggs to temper and then, while whisking the cream mixture, add the eggs in a slow stream. Cook the mixture over medium heat, stirring constantly, until the custard thickens and coats the back of a spoon, or until a thermometer registers 170°. Do not let the mixture boil. Strain the custard through a sieve into a clean metal bowl. Place the bowl in a large bowl of ice water and stir with a metal whisk or spoon until chilled.

Freeze the custard in an ice-cream maker, according to manufacturer's directions. Transfer ice cream to an airtight container and put in freezer to harden, about 2 hours.

WHAT TO DRINK

For this occasion, we turn to South Africa for a couple of wines to match up the variety of flavors. Steen, Afrikaans for stone, is what South Africans call Chenin Blanc. Theirs is a clean, crisp style of white with lovely peach and floral aromas and enough body to stand up to rich foods. Start the night with this wine and continue until the lamb.

For the lamb try out South African Shiraz with its bold, spicy fruit flavors and chewy tannins. Round out your affair with a late harvest Chenin Blanc from South Africa. If the search for one proves difficult, substitute a sweet Chenin Blanc from France's Loire Valley.

MARK ALBA

gives dinner parties to impress on a nightly basis as executive chef of The Food Studio. As a kid, Alba
wanted to be an astronaut but now says: "Being a chef is the only occupation that matters to me.
I wouldn't trade it for any other." Raised in Louisiana, Mark's favorite dishes
to prepare are anything Cajun or Creole.

Finish the sentence: "I wish I could..."
Play the trumpet.
I love jazz music.

What's your most used quote in the kitchen?
"If you're not moving, you're standing still."

If you could have a theme song playing every time you walk into the kitchen, what would it be?
Anything by Rage Against the Machine. They're one of my favorite bands that I listen to a lot. Their music really gets me going.

What would you do if you won the lottery?
I would open "Restaurant ALBA."

If you could cook a meal for anyone, who would it be?
My chef idol, Alfred Portale.

What's your favorite movie?
The Wizard of Oz.

What's your favorite guilty pleasure?
Reese's Peanut Butter Cups or Cheetos.

What's your favorite kitchen tool?
I can't live without my chinois or my Vita-Mix blender.

177

JASON HILL

{ WISTERIA }

Grandmother's Classics with a Twist

Braised Green Mac and Cheese

Corn Pudding

Beef Tenderloin Meatloaf with Roasted Tomatoes

Iron Skillet Fried Chicken

Apple Crisp Cobbler

Braised Green Mac and Cheese

{ Serves 6 to 8 }

2 cups dried elbow macaroni
Kosher salt
1 pound collard, mustard or turnip greens
7 tablespoons unsalted butter, divided, additional for the baking dish
¾ teaspoon finely chopped garlic
2 tablespoons all-purpose flour
2 cups heavy cream
2 teaspoons finely chopped fresh parsley
2 teaspoons finely chopped fresh thyme
1 teaspoon finely chopped fresh sage
½ teaspoon finely chopped fresh rosemary
⅛ teaspoon cayenne pepper
½ teaspoon salt
¼ teaspoon freshly ground pepper
½ pound grated New York sharp cheddar cheese
⅓ cup panko (Japanese breadcrumbs)

~

Heat oven to 350°. Butter a 2½-quart, deep casserole dish and set aside.

Fill a large pot with water. Bring to a boil, add 1 teaspoon salt and the macaroni, reduce heat to a low boil and cook al denté (until it offers a slight resistance when bitten into), about 9 minutes. Empty the macaroni into a colander to drain.

Rinse and remove tough stems from greens. Pat dry and cut into strips. Heat the Dutch oven over medium-high heat. Add 2 tablespoons butter and garlic and heat until butter is melted and garlic is fragrant, about 1 minute. Add greens and cook and gently stir until wilted, about 4 minutes. Add the cooked greens to the macaroni in the colander and drain. In the same Dutch oven, heat 4 tablespoons butter with flour over medium heat and stir for 3 minutes. Gradually add the cream and stir until thickened.

Mix the parsley, thyme, sage and rosemary in a small bowl. Stir the cayenne, salt and pepper and half the herb mixture into the cream sauce. Mix the collards and macaroni into the cream sauce in the Dutch oven.

Spread a layer of greens and pasta mix in the casserole, layer with the cheese, repeating the layers with remaining ingredients until casserole is full. Top with the panko and remaining herbs. Dot the top with remaining butter. Bake until bubbly and golden brown, about 45 minutes.

Corn Pudding

{ Serves 4 to 6 }

¾ cup rice flour
¼ cup granulated sugar
2 teaspoons baking powder
4 cups corn, cut from the cob or frozen, thawed
¼ cup buttermilk
4 tablespoons unsalted butter, melted, additional for the baking dish
2 large eggs, separated
2 ounces Asiago cheese (1 cup shredded)
Kosher salt and freshly ground pepper

~

Preheat oven to 350°. Butter a 12- x 9-inch baking dish and set aside.

In a large bowl, mix flour, sugar and baking powder together. Set aside. In a blender, purée the corn with the buttermilk, melted butter and egg yolks. Add the corn puree to the flour mixture then stir in the grated cheese.

In a stand mixer fitted with the whisk attachment, whip the egg whites to stiff peaks. Gently fold the beaten whites into the corn mixture and season with salt and pepper.

Spread the mixture into the prepared baking dish and bake until golden brown, about 30 minutes. Let stand for 5 minutes before serving.

"I tried to make my first omelet at age four. My mom was very patient with me; she knew I was a perfectionist. I got an omelet pan for Christmas that year."

Beef Tenderloin Meatloaf with Roasted Tomatoes

{ Serves 4 to 6 }

1 pint cherry tomatoes
1 tablespoon olive oil
Kosher salt and freshly ground pepper
1 cup diced onion (about 1 medium onion)
1 tablespoon minced garlic
1 tablespoon finely chopped fresh rosemary
1 tablespoon finely chopped fresh thyme
1 6-ounce can tomato paste (¾ cup)
1 cup diced, stewed tomatoes
2 large eggs, lightly beaten
2 tablespoons Worcestershire sauce
1½ teaspoons ancho chili powder
1½ teaspoons celery salt
2 pounds ground beef tenderloin
1 cup panko (Japanese breadcrumbs)

~

Preheat oven to 250°.

Cut cherry tomatoes in half and place on a rimmed baking sheet. Drizzle with olive oil and lightly sprinkle with salt and pepper. Roast tomatoes until caramelized, about 1½ hours. Set aside and let cool. Increase the oven temperature to 325°.

In a large mixing bowl combine roasted tomatoes, onion, garlic, rosemary, thyme, tomato paste, stewed tomatoes, eggs, Worcestershire, chili powder and celery salt. Mix well. Add the ground beef and panko and mix well.

Place the ground beef mixture onto a rimmed baking sheet and form into a loaf. Bake at 325° for 45 minutes. Remove from the oven and let rest at least 10 minutes before serving.

This is the perfect time to use the trimmings from a whole beef tenderloin. Or, you can ask your butcher for tenderloin trimmings. You'll need a little fat mixed in with the meat.

Iron Skillet Fried Chicken

{ Serves 4 }

3 cups buttermilk
3 tablespoons paprika, divided
1 tablespoon ancho chili powder
¾ teaspoon cayenne, divided
1 fryer chicken, cut into pieces (or select chicken pieces as desired, bone-in and skin-on)
2 cups all-purpose flour
2 tablespoons kosher salt
2 teaspoons white pepper
Canola oil (for frying)

~

In a large bowl, mix the buttermilk with 1 tablespoon paprika, chili powder and ¼ teaspoon cayenne. Whisk until well blended. Add the chicken to the buttermilk mixture and toss and make sure all chicken is well coated. Cover loosely with plastic wrap and let marinate for at least 30 minutes at room temperature or in the refrigerator for up to 24 hours.

Sift the flour, remaining 2 tablespoons paprika and ½ teaspoon cayenne, salt and white pepper into a large shallow plate.

Heat a large, deep, cast iron skillet. Fill half-way with oil and heat the oil to 350°.

Preheat oven to 350°. Place a cooling rack over a rimmed baking sheet and set aside.

Piece by piece, remove the chicken from the marinade. Dredge each piece separately in the flour mixture to coat. Carefully place the chicken in the oil, meat side down, without crowding the pan and working in batches if necessary. Cook until golden brown, about 5 minutes, and turn. Remove cooked chicken to the prepared rack, meat side up, and repeat with remaining chicken. Place chicken in oven and cook until meat thermometer reaches 170°, about 40 minutes.

Apple Crisp Cobbler

{ Serves 6 to 8 }

1 tablespoon butter for the baking dish
6 tart baking apples such as Rome or Granny Smith, cored, peeled and sliced
⅓ cup granulated sugar
½ teaspoon ground cinnamon
¼ teaspoon ground cloves
1 teaspoon vanilla extract
1 teaspoon lemon juice
1 cup all-purpose flour
¾ cup rolled oats
¾ cup dark brown sugar, firmly packed
¼ teaspoon fine salt
8 tablespoons cold, unsalted butter, cut into small pieces

~

Preheat oven to 350°. Butter a 1½-quart baking dish and set aside.

In a medium saucepan, mix apples with sugar, cinnamon, cloves, vanilla extract and lemon juice. Cook over medium heat just until tender, about 8 minutes.

While the apples are cooking, make the topping. In a large bowl, mix the flour, oats, brown sugar and salt until well blended. Cut in the butter with a pastry cutter (or 2 knives) until the mixture is thoroughly mixed.

Evenly spread apple mixture into the prepared baking dish. Loosely sprinkle the oat mixture over the top. Bake until bubbly and starting to brown, about 30 minutes.

WHAT TO DRINK

Flavors of the South require a wine with considerable backbone and depth. Argentina has found its mark with their robust Malbecs. This inky red is called "black wine" in France where it is still made in the southwest region of Cahors. The color is dark as night, but the flavors are of bright red fruits with an elegant touch of earth. The wine should hold up with the rich fried chicken, while having the elegance and grace to partner with the tenderloin meatloaf. Round out the meal with a glass of Calvados, France's supreme apple brandy.

JASON HILL

says his meals at home growing up were very Southern—a lot of meatloaf, baked potatoes and green beans. When his grandmother prepared dinner at her house, it was a full spread with at least 40 items on the table. Now, at Wisteria, Jason creates modernized versions of comfort foods and old favorites. Jason says, "My most memorable moment was the way my mother looked at me when Wisteria started doing well— like she was finally really proud."

Finish the sentence: "I wish I could..."
Afford older cars to collect, especially pre-70s automobiles.

If you could cook a meal for anyone, who would it be?
Any of the pro golfers at the Masters on the first day of the event, so Jack Nicklaus and Sam Snead would be there.

What are your favorite guilty pleasures?
Good wine, ice cream and giving gifts.

What are four movies you could watch over and over?
Stripes, Star Wars, True Romance and *Frosty the Snowman*.

What would you do if you won the lottery?
Call my mom and tell her to retire. Help all my friends pay off their debt. Then do all the traveling that I haven't had time to do.

What's something that people would be surprised to know about you?
I can arrange flowers and I love to shop.

If you could have a theme song playing every time you walk into the kitchen, what would it be?
"Love on the Rocks" by Neil Diamond.

As a kid, what did you want to be when you grew up?
Pele.

NICK OLTARSH

LOBBY AT TWELVE

Sunday Brunch for Friends

Buttermilk Pancakes with Peach Melba and Sugared Walnuts

Gravlax Twirls with Dijon-Dill Sauce

Hot Smoked Salmon and Zucchini Fritatta

Steel Cut Oatmeal with Mulled Dates, Vanilla Sugar and Dried Apricots

Breakfast Buttermilk Panna Cotta

Buttermilk Pancakes with Peach Melba and Sugared Walnuts

{ Serves 4 }

PEACH MELBA
2 pints fresh strawberries, hulled and sliced
1 fresh peach, pitted and sliced
1 cup granulated sugar
¼ cup lemon juice

SUGARED WALNUTS
2 tablespoons water
2 tablespoons granulated sugar,
    more for sprinkling
1 cup walnuts

PANCAKES
1 cup all-purpose flour
2 tablespoons granulated sugar
½ teaspoon baking soda
½ teaspoon salt
1 cup buttermilk
2 tablespoons unsalted butter, melted
1 large egg, lightly beaten
Canola oil, for cooking
Maple syrup, for serving
Clotted or Devonshire cream, for garnish

~

PEACH MELBA In a small saucepan, combine the strawberries, peach, sugar and lemon juice. Bring to a boil, reduce heat and, stirring continuously, cook for 1 minute. Remove the pan from heat and cool.

SUGARED WALNUTS Preheat oven to 300°. Line a rimmed baking sheet with a non-stick silicone baking sheet; set aside. In a small saucepan, mix 2 tablespoons water and 2 tablespoons sugar together and bring to a boil. Remove from the heat. Stir the walnuts in the sugar syrup until well coated. Remove the walnuts from the syrup with a slotted spoon. Spread evenly on the prepared baking sheet and sprinkle with additional sugar to coat. Place in oven and bake until fragrant and golden brown, 5-6 minutes.

PANCAKES Sift flour, sugar, baking soda and salt into a large bowl. In a large measuring cup combine the buttermilk, melted butter and egg. Add the wet ingredients to the dry and gently stir in; do not over mix, some lumps are fine. Heat a griddle or large skillet over medium heat. Brush with canola oil. Ladle pancake batter onto hot griddle to form several small pancakes. Cook until bubbles start to form on the top surface and the surface begins to dry, about 3 minutes. With a thin, offset spatula, flip the pancakes and cook until golden on the other side, an additional 2-3 minutes.

To serve, place pancakes on a warm plate, top with peach melba and sugared walnuts, add a dollop of clotted cream and serve with a side of maple syrup.

Gravlax Twirls with Dijon-Dill Sauce

{ Serves 10 }

3 tablespoons granulated sugar
3 tablespoons kosher salt
3 tablespoons finely chopped fresh dill
½ pound salmon filet, skin on

~

Salmon needs 2 days to cure so plan ahead.

In a small bowl, mix sugar, salt and dill. Lay out a large piece of plastic wrap on a counter. Sprinkle half the sugar mixture on the plastic wrap. Place the salmon filet on top. Sprinkle the remaining sugar mixture on top of the salmon spreading it to cover the entire surface. Fold and wrap the salmon with the plastic wrap and place on a rimmed baking sheet, as the salmon will weep moisture as it cures. Place another baking sheet on top of the salmon and weigh down with a heavy cast iron pan or cans. Place in the refrigerator and let the salmon cure for at least 48 hours.

Remove the salmon from the refrigerator and remove weights. Rinse the cured salmon under cold running water to remove the marinade. Pat dry with paper towels. Put the salmon, skin side down, on a cutting board and, with a sharp slicing knife, slice the salmon on an angle across the grain, as thinly as possible leaving the skin on the board. Twirl each strip of salmon decoratively around a small fork and drizzle with dijon-dill sauce; serve right from the fork. Garnish with dill sprigs. Alternately, roll salmon pinwheel fashion and place on a piece of cucumber. Drizzle with sauce and garnish with dill.

DIJON-DILL SAUCE

¼ cup Dijon mustard
2 tablespoons sugar
3 tablespoons red wine vinegar
½ teaspoon kosher salt
1 cup canola oil
2 tablespoons finely chopped fresh dill

~

In a small bowl, whisk mustard, sugar, vinegar and salt until well blended. Gradually whisk in canola oil in a slow steady stream. Add dill. If sauce is too thick, whisk in a tablespoon of water to thin.

Oltarsh grew up in New York City and eventually attended the University of Pennsylvania to study French literature.

Hot Smoked Salmon and Zucchini Frittata

{ Serves 6 }

½ small zucchini, cut on the diagonal into ⅓-inch slices
1 tablespoon extra virgin olive oil
⅓ cup chopped sun-dried tomatoes
1 tablespoon unsalted butter
1 tablespoon finely diced onion
4 large eggs
1 tablespoon heavy cream
1 ounce hot smoked salmon, flaked
Kosher salt and freshly ground pepper to taste
1 tablespoon crème fraîche
Dill sprigs, for garnish

~

Preheat oven to 500°. Brush the zucchini with the olive oil and season with salt and pepper. Heat a grill, grill pan or large skillet to high. Add the zucchini and cook until it just begins to soften, about 2 minutes. Set aside.

Place the sun-dried tomatoes in a little water in a small glass bowl or measuring cup. Heat the tomatoes in the microwave until boiling, about 1 minute. Set aside to plump and reconstitute. Melt the butter over low heat in an oven-proof, 8-inch non-stick skillet. Increase the heat to medium and add the diced onions and well-drained sun-dried tomatoes. Cook until the onions become translucent, about 1 minute. In a large bowl, whisk the eggs and the cream together. Add the eggs to the onion/tomato mixture. With a heat resistant spatula, push the cooked eggs towards the center of the pan as they cook and let the uncooked eggs fill in any empty space. When the eggs are starting to set, spread the salmon and cooked zucchini over the top. Place the skillet in the oven for 5 minutes, or until eggs are set. Carefully remove the hot skillet from the oven, season to taste with salt and pepper, and garnish with a large dollop of crème fraîche and fresh dill sprigs.

Steel Cut Oatmeal with Mulled Dates, Vanilla Sugar and Dried Apricots

{ Serves 4 to 6 }

½ cup whole milk
6 cups water
1 tablespoon unsalted butter
¼ cup brown sugar
Pinch kosher salt
1¼ cups steel cut oats
1 stick cinnamon, broken in pieces
1 sprig thyme

1 piece star anise
1 cup Medjool dates, pitted and quartered
½-¾ cup red wine (to cover)
¼ cup granulated sugar
¼ teaspoon ground allspice
Vanilla Bean Sugar, for serving
Heavy cream, for serving
Dried apricots, diced, for serving

~

Combine the milk, water, butter, brown sugar and a pinch of salt in a medium saucepan and bring to a boil. When boiling, slowly stir in the oats. Reduce the heat to simmer and cook until tender and the oatmeal thickens, 30-40 minutes.

Meanwhile, prepare the mulled dates. Make a spice bundle of cinnamon pieces, thyme and star anise in a piece of cheesecloth and tie with string. Place the dates in a heavy-bottom saucepan with enough red wine to cover. Add the sugar, allspice and the spice bundle and bring to a boil. Boil for 1 minute. Using a slotted spoon, remove the chopped dates and transfer to a small bowl. Continue to cook the remaining liquid until reduced, 4-5 minutes. Remove the spice bundle and pour the reduced liquid over the dates. Keep warm for serving.

To serve, pour the hot oatmeal into warm serving bowls. Top with warm mulled dates, vanilla sugar to taste, heavy cream and apricots.

VANILLA BEAN SUGAR

1 whole vanilla bean
3 cups granulated sugar

~

Split the vanilla bean in half lengthwise and place in an airtight container with the sugar. Prepare vanilla sugar in advance; the longer the vanilla bean is in the sugar, the more the vanilla essence infuses the sugar. This makes more vanilla sugar than is needed for this recipe, but vanilla sugar has other uses such as sprinkled over fresh berries, or in cookies, cakes, and beverages.

"While I was at Lespinasse there was such an incredibly high standard for everything we did . . . it really set the stage for my future career."

Breakfast Buttermilk Panna Cotta

{ Serves 8 }

2¼ cups heavy cream
1¼ cups sugar
4 ¼-ounce envelopes powdered gelatin
3¼ cups buttermilk
1 pint fresh strawberries
1 pint fresh blackberries
1 pint golden raspberries
8 sprigs of fresh mint

In a 2-quart saucepan, bring heavy cream and sugar to a full boil and stir to dissolve the sugar.

Place the gelatin powder into a large bowl, preferably with a spout. Pour hot cream and sugar mixture over gelatin and stir until the gelatin dissolves completely. Add buttermilk and stir until incorporated.

Pour the warm panna cotta mixture into 8 decorative glasses filling each glass approximately one-half full (ice tea or large martini glasses are perfect). Cover each glass individually with plastic wrap or waxed paper. Place the glasses in the refrigerator and let them sit for at least 6 hours or overnight.

In a colander rinse strawberries, blackberries and raspberries under cool water. Remove the stem and core from the strawberries and cut in half. Fold the blackberries and raspberries into the strawberries. Just before serving, top each glass of panna cotta with the mixed berries and garnish each with a mint sprig.

WHAT TO DRINK

Nothing defines brunch better than a mimosa. Try using Spanish cava as the base for this classic beverage for your next late-morning get together. To add flair to the occasion, splash a touch of blended fresh berries into the OJ and sparkler. Your guests will never forget.

knew he wanted to be a chef from day one. He started his own catering company in high school – Putting on the Ritz. He would cater parties for family friends and even traded one dinner party for professional business cards. Oltarsh's parents were wonderful cooks, inspiring him from early on. "My mother was a fabulous home cook and my grandmother had an incredible food sensibility." Nick credits Gray Kunz, the chef of Lespinasse in New York City, with being most inspirational to his culinary career.

What is your favorite guilty pleasure?
Definitely movies.
I love watching movies.

Finish the sentence: "I wish I could..."
Travel the world. I would love to visit Asia and Angkor Wat in Cambodia.

What's your favorite place to eat when you're not at your own restaurant?
Fogo de Chão.

What's your most used quote in the kitchen?
"The road to hell is paved with good intentions."

What movies could you watch over and over again?
Carmen, Risky Business, Eat Drink Man Woman, and *Notting Hill.*

What accomplishment are you most proud of?
I finished the *New York Times* crossword puzzle, without cheating.

If you could have a theme song playing every time you walk into the kitchen, what would it be?
"Tragedy" by the Bee Gees.

What's something that people would be surprised to know about you?
I hate Big Red chewing gum.

BARB PIRES

METROTAINMENT BAKERY

Just Desserts

Sugar Free Carrot Cake with Sugar Free Cream Cheese Frosting

Pineapple Cloud

Pear Almond Pound Cake

Chocolate Gran Marnier Pâté with Butter Wafers

Coconut Cake

Sugar Free Carrot Cake
with Sugar Free Cream Cheese Frosting

{ Makes 1 2-layer 8-inch cake }

1½ cups all-purpose flour
1½ cups Splenda sugar substitute
¾ teaspoon baking soda
¾ teaspoon baking powder
¾ teaspoon ground cinnamon
½ teaspoon iodized salt

¾ cup vegetable or canola oil
3 large eggs, lightly beaten
2¼ cups finely grated carrots (4 carrots)
1¼ cups walnuts, divided
Sugar Free Cream Cheese Frosting

~

Preheat oven to 350°. Spray 2 (8-inch) cake pans with non-stick spray and set aside.

In a stand mixer fitted with a paddle attachment, combine the flour, Splenda, baking soda, baking powder, cinnamon and salt. Turn the mixer on low speed to combine ingredients. With the mixer running, add the oil and eggs and mix on low speed until well combined. Turn the mixer off and scrape down the sides and bottom of the bowl with a rubber spatula. Add carrots and ½ cup of chopped walnuts and mix on low speed until combined, about 1 minute.

Divide the cake batter evenly between the pans. Place the cakes on rack in center of the oven and bake for 30 minutes. Test for doneness by inserting a cake tester or toothpick in center of the cake, when it comes out clean, the cakes are done.

Remove the cakes from the oven and cool, in the pans, on a wire rack for 10 minutes. Remove the cakes from pans and place on cooling rack. When cakes have completely cooled, spread each with a layer of frosting and stack one on top of the other. Frost the sides with the remaining frosting. Finely chop the remaining ¼ cup of walnuts and press into the sides of the cake, coming up over the top, leaving a 3-inch circle in the center with no nuts.

SUGAR FREE CREAM CHEESE FROSTING

8 tablespoons (1 stick) unsalted butter, chilled and cut into cubes
12 ounces cream cheese, chilled and cut into cubes
1½ teaspoons pure vanilla extract
½ cup Splenda sugar substitute

~

In a stand mixer fitted with the paddle attachment, beat the butter on medium-high until smooth. Add cream cheese and vanilla and continue beating until smooth and fluffy. Reduce the speed of the mixer to low and gradually add the Splenda, beating until frosting is smooth and creamy.

Pineapple Cloud

{ Makes 1 9-inch cake }

1 angel food cake
2 cups heavy whipping cream
1¾ cups granulated sugar, divided
12 ounces cream cheese (cold)
1 teaspoon vanilla extract
1 20-ounce can unsweetened, crushed pineapple, drained well, divided

~

Place the bowl and whisk for the stand mixer in the freezer to chill.

Using a serrated knife, slice the angel food cake into ¼-inch slices. Cut each slice into 3 pieces. Place the slices in a 9-inch spring form pan, covering the bottom and standing pieces up the sides; set aside. (Reserve remaining cake for later use.)

Remove the bowl and whisk from the freezer. In a stand mixer fitted with the whisk attachment, whip the cream on high speed, until soft peaks form. Add ¾ cup sugar and beat just until stiff peaks form, about 30 seconds. Remove the whipped cream to another bowl and refrigerate.

In the stand mixer fitted with the whisk attachment, in the same bowl, beat the cream cheese until smooth. Slowly add 1 cup sugar and the vanilla extract and mix on medium-high speed until smooth, about 2 minutes. Reduce the speed to low and add ¾ cup of the pineapple, just until blended. Using a large rubber spatula, gently fold the whipped cream into the pineapple cream cheese mixture.

Spread a layer of the cream cheese mixture in the prepared spring form pan, add the remaining angel food cake slices and then spread with the remaining cream cheese mixture. Sprinkle the remaining pineapple on the top of the cake. Cover with plastic wrap and chill overnight.

To serve, carefully open the spring and remove the sides from the spring form pan. Slide the cake onto a cake stand and refrigerate until ready to serve. Slice with a serrated knife and serve immediately.

Pear Almond Pound Cake

{ Makes one Bundt or tube pan }

3 cups all-purpose flour
3 cups sugar
1 teaspoon baking powder
½ teaspoon iodized salt
⅛ teaspoon ground cinnamon
1 cup whole milk
1¼ cups vegetable oil
2 large eggs, lightly beaten
2 teaspoons vanilla extract
1 cup slivered almonds
1 28-ounce can Bartlett pears, drained and diced
Glaze

~

Preheat oven to 325°. Spray baking pan with cooking spray and set aside.

In a stand mixer fitted with the paddle attachment, combine flour, sugar, baking powder, salt and cinnamon on low speed. With the mixer running, add the milk, oil, eggs and vanilla extract. Stir in almonds. Turn the mixer off and scrape down the sides and bottom of the bowl. Adjust the speed on the mixer to medium and beat for 2 minutes until all ingredients are combined.

Pour the batter into the prepared pan and bake on the center rack of the oven for 1 hour. Place a cooling rack on a rimmed baking sheet and set aside. Test the cake for doneness by inserting a cake tester or toothpick in center of the cake. When the tester comes out clean, remove the cake from the oven and place the pan on the prepared rack. Cool for about 10 minutes and run a knife between the edges of the cake and the pan, loosening the cake. Carefully turn out onto the wire rack and tap the bottom of the pan to release the cake onto the cooling rack. Insert a wooden skewer to make holes in the top of the cake and drizzle the glaze over the top. Repeat the process until the cake is well glazed. Let the cake come to room temperature to set the glaze. Slice and serve.

GLAZE

¼ cup whole milk
1 cup light brown sugar, firmly packed
½ cup (1 stick) unsalted butter

~

In a heavy-bottom 1-quart saucepan combine milk, brown sugar and butter. Cook over medium-high heat, stirring frequently until sugar dissolves and mixture comes to a boil. Keep the mixture warm on low heat, stirring occasionally.

Chocolate Grand Marnier Pâté with Butter Wafers

{ Serves 6 }

2 cups semisweet chocolate chips
¾ cup heavy whipping cream
3 ounces cream cheese
2 tablespoons Grand Marnier
Berries for garnish
Whipped cream for garnish
Butter Wafers

~

Place chocolate and heavy cream in a glass bowl and melt in microwave using medium (or "melt") setting, stirring often, until smooth. In a separate bowl, with a hand mixer on low setting, beat the cream cheese until smooth. Add the chocolate mixture to the cheese and mix on low until smooth. Slowly add the Grand Marnier and mix until well-blended. Pour mixture into a small (4- x 8-inch) loaf pan lined with plastic wrap. Chill overnight. Remove the loaf from the pan, using the edges of the plastic wrap to lift the pâté out. Invert on a cutting board and slice with a smooth edged slicing knife that has been dipped in very hot water. Wipe the blade and dip in hot water before each cut. Serve with fresh berries and a dollop of whipped cream. Serve butter wafer on the side.

BUTTER WAFERS

½ pound unsalted butter (2 sticks), chilled
½ cup granulated sugar
1 large egg, lightly beaten
1 teaspoon pure vanilla extract
2 cups all-purpose flour, additional for flouring board
1 teaspoon baking powder
Pinch of salt

~

In the bowl of a stand mixer fitted with the paddle attachment, cream butter on high until light and fluffy, about 3 minutes. Gradually add sugar and beat until creamy, light and fluffy. Add egg and vanilla and beat until well combined. Turn the mixer to lowest setting and add flour, baking powder and salt. Mix on low speed just until combined. Wrap dough into a 1½-inch cylinder in plastic wrap and refrigerate to chill and harden for 30 minutes or longer.

Preheat oven to 350°. When dough has firmed up, remove from the refrigerator. Dust a clean counter with flour and remove the plastic wrap from the dough. With a sharp, straight bladed knife that has been dipped in very hot water, slice the dough into ½-inch thick wafers. Place on a rimmed baking sheet and bake 8-10 minutes, or until edges are lightly brown. Remove from cookie sheet and cool on a wire rack.

Coconut Cake

{ Makes a 3-layer 9-inch cake or a 4-layer 8-inch cake }

½ cup (1 stick) unsalted butter
½ cup shortening
5 large eggs, separated and divided
2 cups sugar
2 cups flour
1 teaspoon baking soda
¼ teaspoon salt
1 cup buttermilk
1½ teaspoons pure vanilla extract
5 egg whites
¾ cup Coco Lopez (sweetened cream of coconut)
Cream Cheese Frosting
2 cups sweetened, flaked coconut

~

Preheat oven to 350°. Spray 3 9-inch cake pans (or 2 deep 8-inch cake pans) with non-stick spray. Alternately, cut a piece of wax or parchment to fit the bottom of each pan. Grease the pans, bottom and sides, place the cut paper in the bottom of the pans and then gently grease and flour the paper. Set aside.

In a stand mixer fitted with the paddle attachment, combine butter, shortening, yolks and sugar on medium speed until light and fluffy, about 5 minutes. Turn the mixer off and scrape down sides and bottom of bowl several times during beating. In a separate bowl, sift flour, soda, and salt together. With the mixer on low speed, alternately add flour mixture and buttermilk to butter/shortening mixture, starting and ending with flour. Turn the mixer off and scrape down sides and bottom of bowl several times.

In a clean mixer bowl, in the stand mixer fitted with the whisk attachment, beat the egg whites on high to soft peaks. Add vanilla and beat to stiff but not dry peaks. Alternately, you can beat the whites in a bowl with a handheld mixer.

With a large rubber spatula, gently fold the beaten whites into the batter. Divide the batter between the prepared pans. Evenly space the cake pans in the center of the oven and bake for 25 minutes. Test for doneness by inserting a cake tester or toothpick in center of the cake, when it comes out clean, the cakes are done.

"My grandmother used to take me downtown on Saturdays and we would go to a local bakery and watch the lady in the window frost cakes. It was the highlight of my week."

Remove from the oven and cool, in the pans, on a wire rack for 10 minutes. Remove from pans and place on cooling rack. If you made 2 layers, carefully split each layer through the center, making a total of 4 layers.

When layers have cooled, slowly drizzle and spread a thin layer of Coco Lopez over each layer and allow to absorb. Do not soak the layers.

Frost each layer and then stack, one on top of the other. Frost sides of the now 3-layer cake. Sprinkle the coconut over the top and gently pat the coconut into the sides of the cake.

CREAM CHEESE FROSTING

1 cup (2 sticks) unsalted butter, chilled and cut into cubes
16 ounces cream cheese, chilled and cut into cubes
2 teaspoons vanilla extract
7½ cups sifted 10x confectioners' sugar (almost 2 1-pound boxes)

~

In a stand mixer fitted with the paddle attachment, beat the butter on medium-high until smooth. Add cream cheese and vanilla extract and continue beating until smooth and fluffy. Reduce the speed of the mixer to low and gradually add the powdered sugar, beating until frosting is smooth and creamy.

WHAT TO DRINK

For desserts the options are more varied than most tend to think. There are a few rules of thumb to keep in mind to make the selection easy and the pairing work. Chocolate desserts are superb with late harvest and botrytis wines such as Sauternes, Montbazillac, and Barsac. Chocolate makes for a great dance partner with port as well.

Panna cotta, crème brûlée and other cream-based classics call for a lighter sweetness like that delivered in Demi-sec Champagnes and Italian moscatos. Fall spices and flavors like those found in pumpkin pie, carrot cake and apple crumble as well as nut-based treats like pecan pie and baklava call for dense, concentrated flavors. Tuscany's famed Vin Santo exudes rich raisin flavors, which complement the earthy spices of these desserts. Additionally, Hungary's Tokaji nectar stimulates the palate in ways unimaginable.

Sparkling wine's effervescent character lets the tiny bubbles mingle with fresh fruit on the palate making a tingly sensation that is to die for. And for tropical fruits like pineapple and passion fruit, complex late harvest wines such as Alsace's Gewürztraminer and Pinot Gris bring added tropical character to the table.

was hired in 1998 to create and bake quality desserts at an affordable price for all of the restaurants owned by Metrotainment Cafes. The bakery started out in a small space within Einstein's on Juniper Street, then expanded to a spot on Crescent Avenue a year later and finally found its forever home on 14th Street. Barb makes desserts for restaurants throughout the city, bakes cakes for brides and corporate clients, and opened a retail bakery for those in the neighborhood.

Who is a famous person you've cooked for?
Jimmy Carter, a few years ago for his birthday celebration at the Carter Center.

What four movies could you watch over and over?
Lonesome Dove, Pretty Woman, Finding Neverland and *Braveheart*.

What's your most used quote in the kitchen?
"That's beautiful!"

What songs never get old to you?
Anything by the Beatles.

What's your favorite drink?
Bloody Marys or margaritas.

What words do you live by?
"No excuses."

What was the first dish you learned how to cook?
Brownies.

What's something that people would be surprised to know about you?
I have never been to culinary school and I have a degree in psychology.

What is your all-time favorite movie?
Peter Pan.

Where would you like to visit that you've never been before?
Greece.

CRAIG RICHARDS

Romantic Italian Dinner

Seared Scallops with Sweet Pea Puree and Brown Butter

Beet and Nectarine Salad with Shaved Fennel
and Goat Cheese

Risotto with Spring Herbs and Asparagus

Flounder Involtini with Yukon Potato Puree

Chocolate Crema with Marinated Strawberries

Seared Scallops with Sweet Pea Puree and Brown Butter

{ Serves 2 }

1 cup shelled English peas
3 tablespoons extra virgin olive oil, divided
Kosher salt and freshly ground pepper
4 sea scallops
1 tablespoon unsalted butter
1 tablespoon capers, rinsed
2 sprigs fresh thyme, for garnish

Bring a pot of lightly salted water to a boil. Prepare a large bowl of ice water and keep it nearby. Add peas and blanch in salted water for two minutes. Drain the peas into a colander. Place colander in an ice water bath to stop the cooking process. (This is called "shocking.") When peas have cooled, remove the colander from the ice water and drain. Add peas, 1 tablespoon olive oil and 2 tablespoons of cooking water to a blender. Blend until smooth, adding more cooking water as needed to make a smooth puree. Season to taste with a generous amount of salt; set aside.

Heat a sauté pan over medium-high heat and add remaining 2 tablespoons olive oil. Season scallops with salt and pepper. When olive oil begins to smoke, add scallops. Cook for two minutes and turn. Cook for an additional two minutes and check for doneness. The scallops should be crispy on the outside and springy to the touch. Remove scallops from the sauté pan and drain on a plate lined with a paper towel.

Add butter, capers and thyme to the sauté pan and cook over medium-high heat until butter is a nutty brown color and capers start to split.

To serve, spoon puree onto two warm plates and top with scallops. Spoon brown butter sauce on top of scallops and around plate. Garnish with fresh thyme and serve immediately.

Beet and Nectarine Salad with Shaved Fennel and Goat Cheese

{ Serves 4 }

3 medium red and gold beets
1 ripe nectarine
1 small bulb fresh fennel
¼ cup Red Wine Vinaigrette
1 small bunch frisée, cleaned
4 ounces soft fresh goat cheese

~

Preheat oven to 350°. Wrap beets individually in aluminum foil and cook in oven for 1 hour, or until fork tender. Cool in the aluminum foil to room temperature. (The beets will steam in the foil, making it very easy to remove the skin.) Remove the skin, cut the beets into ½-inch cubes and place in a medium bowl.

Cut the nectarine in half, remove the pit and cut into ¼-inch wedges and add to the beets. Halve the fennel and remove core. Shave fennel crosswise on a mandoline into the beet mixture. Add the red wine vinaigrette with a pinch of salt and stir to combine; set aside.

Using a slotted spoon remove the beet mixture from the red wine vinaigrette (which will be bright red due to the beets). Add the frisée and toss to coat. To serve, divide the frisée between four plates and top with the reserved beet mixture. Crumble the goat cheese around each salad and drizzle with a little more of the beet-infused red wine vinaigrette.

RED WINE VINAIGRETTE

2 tablespoons red wine vinegar
¼ teaspoon granulated sugar
Kosher salt and freshly ground pepper
⅓ cup extra virgin olive oil

~

Combine vinegar, sugar, a pinch of salt and pepper in a bowl. Whisking constantly, slowly drizzle in the olive oil until vinaigrette is well blended. Taste and adjust the seasoning with salt and pepper.

"If I could cook for anyone, it'd be
Michael Stipe of R.E.M."

Risotto with Spring Herbs and Asparagus

{ Serves 4 to 6 }

¼ pound fresh asparagus
4 cups chicken stock (or low sodium broth)
¼ cup extra virgin olive oil
½ cup finely diced onion
1 cup Arborio rice
¼ cup dry white wine
¼ cup finely chopped mixed herbs (basil, marjoram, thyme, parsley, oregano)
¼ cup fresh grated Parmigiano-Reggiano cheese
2 tablespoons unsalted butter
Kosher salt and black or white pepper

～

Remove tough ends from asparagus and cut tips and tender stalks into 1-inch pieces. Bring a large pot of salted water to a boil and blanch the asparagus in the boiling water for 2 minutes. Remove to an ice bath (bowl of ice and water) to "shock" (stop the cooking). Remove the blanched asparagus to paper towel lined plate to drain. Discard blanching water.

In the same pot, heat the chicken stock to a low simmer over medium-high heat. In a heavy-bottom Dutch oven, heat the olive oil over medium-high heat. Add the onions and cook until slightly translucent, about 3 minutes. Stir in the rice, making sure it is well coated with oil. Cook until the rice starts to crackle and turns opaque, about 2 minutes. Add the wine and a pinch of salt and stir to coat the rice. Keep stirring and cooking the rice until all the liquid has been absorbed. Stir stock into rice in ½ cup increments, stirring and waiting until the liquid is absorbed before adding the next bit of stock. Stir constantly to avoid sticking. When the stock is almost used up, test for doneness. When the rice is done it will be moist and creamy with a slight bite. Fold in the asparagus, fresh herbs, cheese and butter and season to taste with salt and freshly ground pepper. Serve immediately.

"When it comes to butter, the more the merrier."

Flounder Involtini with Yukon Potato Puree

{ Serves 4 }

2 Yukon gold potatoes
3 tablespoons unsalted butter, cut into pieces
4 tablespoons extra virgin olive oil, divided
4 4-ounce flounder filets (can also use sole)
3 leaves fresh basil, finely chopped
1 zucchini, sliced in long thin spears on a
    mandoline, discarding the seeds
1 tablespoon seasoned breadcrumbs

½ cup dry white wine
1 teaspoon dried red pepper flakes
3 sprigs fresh thyme
1 tablespoon preserved lemons, finely
    chopped, additional for garnish
1 tablespoon finely chopped Italian parsley
Kosher salt and freshly ground pepper

~

Peel the potatoes and place in a large saucepan. Add enough water to completely cover the potatoes. Season with salt and bring to a boil and cook until fork tender, about 30 minutes. Remove and reserve 1 cup of the cooking liquid and drain the potatoes. Return the potatoes to the pan and cook, stirring constantly to evaporate any remaining moisture, 1-2 minutes. Add 2 tablespoons butter, 2 tablespoons of the olive oil and if necessary, a little of the reserved cooking water and purée using a handheld mixer until smooth and easily blended. Season with salt and pepper to taste; set aside and keep warm.

Preheat oven to 450°. Lay flounder filets flat and season one side with salt. Sprinkle with basil and stack a few zucchini spears crosswise in the middle of each filet. Roll fish around zucchini (the spears will stick out each end of the fish roll-up) and top each filet with seasoned breadcrumbs.

Arrange filets in an oblong 2-quart baking dish. Drizzle each with the remaining 2 tablespoons of olive oil. Add wine, red pepper flakes, thyme sprigs, and preserved lemons to the dish and around the filets. Bake in preheated oven until the breadcrumbs are toasted and the fish is cooked through, about 8 minutes. Strain the pan juices into a small saucepan and heat over medium heat. Whisk in remaining 1 tablespoon butter and parsley. To serve, divide potato puree between four warm plates. Arrange fish on top of the puree and spoon sauce around the plate. Garnish with additional preserved lemon.

PRESERVED LEMON

{ Makes about ¼ cup }

1 lemon, very thinly sliced, preferably on a mandoline
¼ cup sugar
¼ salt
½ cup extra virgin olive oil

~

In a medium non-reactive stainless steel or glass bowl combine lemon, sugar and salt; stir to combine. Set aside for 20 minutes. Add olive oil to cover. Marinate overnight at room temperature. Store in an airtight container at room temperature for up to 1 week.

Chocolate Crema with Marinated Strawberries

{ Serves 8 }

½ cup plus 2 tablespoons granulated sugar
1 tablespoon cornstarch
5 large eggs, divided
½ cup whole milk
½ cup heavy cream

8 ounces bittersweet chocolate
Marinated Strawberries
½ cup heavy cream whipped to soft peaks
   with 2 tablespoons granulated sugar

~

In a large bowl, sift together 2 tablespoons sugar and cornstarch and set aside. Separate eggs with yolks in one bowl and whites reserved for later use. Gently stir egg yolks in a small bowl to break yolks. In a medium saucepan, heat milk and cream over medium-high heat. Bring just to a boil and decrease heat. Whisk in sugar/cornstarch mixture. Temper eggs (add a small amount of the warm milk mixture to the eggs and stir to warm the eggs so they do not "cook"). Whisk the now-warm egg yolks slowly into the milk mixture. Cook and continue stirring with a wooden spoon until pudding-like consistency. Remove from heat. Stir in chocolate until melted and set aside to cool.

In a stand mixer fitted with the whip attachment, beat egg whites on high until frothy and gradually add ½ cup sugar until stiff peaks form and mixture is glossy. Fold a little of the whites gently into chocolate mixture to lighten and then fold the chocolate mixture into the whites until completely combined. Fill decorative glasses or ramekins three-fourths full with the chocolate. Cover each dish with plastic wrap and chill. Top each dish of crema with a generous tablespoon of berries and a dollop of whipped cream.

MARINATED STRAWBERRIES

1 cup red wine, light to medium-bodied with lots of fruit
Generous ½ cup granulated sugar
½ pint strawberries, stemmed and quartered

Combine wine and sugar in a small saucepan and bring to a boil. Reduce heat and simmer until reduced by two-thirds, about 20 minutes. Remove from heat and allow to cool. Add strawberries and marinate for one hour. If you are not going to use the strawberries immediately, place the mixture in the refrigerator. They will keep up to 12 hours.

WHAT TO DRINK

What is more romantic than sparkling wine? Get the fires burning with a light Prosecco to match the beet salad and linger through the seared scallops. Turn up the heat with the world's most romantic sparkler, Brut Champagne. Keep the party going by adding a splash of Crème de Cassis liqueur to the champagne flute for a Kir Royale, which should help to pair the wine with the chocolate.

CRAIG RICHARDS

came to La Tavola Trattoria in May 2005 after training for five years under the renowned first lady of Italian cuisine, Lidia Bastianich. Her invaluable knowledge of the Italian-American kitchen provided Craig his basic training in the genre. Craig began his culinary career in 1998 at Pachamama's restaurant in Kansas and from there, he took the culinary world by storm at Lidia's Kansas City working his way up from senior line cook to sous chef. In 2001, Richards moved to Pittsburgh to open Lidia's Pittsburgh as executive chef.

What's your favorite movie?
Fight Club.

If you could have a different job for a day, what would it be?
A writer.

What's your favorite book?
Thoreau's *Walden*.

What songs never get old to you?
R.E.M.'s "Gardening at Night" and U2's "New Year's Day."

What's your favorite drink?
Stella Artois beer.

If you could have a theme song playing every time you walk into the kitchen, what would it be?
"Talk" by Coldplay.

What's the strangest ingredient you've ever cooked with?
Pickled lamb's tongue.

What's the strangest thing you've ever seen in a restaurant?
A sommelier making an impromptu potpourri and walking it around the room to perfume the restaurant.

Where do you like to eat when you're not at your own restaurant?
Watershed.

Why do you enjoy cooking?
Because it involves split second timing and adrenaline rushes.

What words do you live by?
Be honest, be humble.

JOE AHN

SOHO

Sliders and Sandwiches

—

Reef and Beef Slider

Lump Crab Cake and Fried Green Tomato on a Biscuit

Asian Slider Burger

Mini Oyster and Crawfish Po' Boy

Italian Mini

Reef and Beef Slider

{ Serves 4 }

½ cup extra virgin olive oil, additional for grill
1 teaspoon chopped garlic
½ teaspoon dried oregano
¼ teaspoon crushed red pepper
2 tablespoons freshly squeezed lemon juice
1 tablespoon finely minced fresh parsley
4-ounce piece filet mignon
4 fresh jumbo shrimp
1 Roma tomato, sliced ¼-inch thick
¼ cup mayonnaise
½ teaspoon chopped garlic
1 teaspoon lemon zest
2 leaves Romaine lettuce, finely shredded
4 3-inch diameter mini hard rolls

~

In a small bowl, whisk oil, garlic, oregano, red pepper, lemon juice and parsley to combine.
Divide into 3 shallow dishes and separately marinate the filet, shrimp and tomatoes for one hour.
In a small bowl, combine mayonnaise, garlic and lemon zest with a small whisk.

Heat a grill or grill pan over medium-high heat and brush with oil. Grill shrimp and steak for
about 3 minutes per side. Grill the tomato last as it just needs about 1 minute per side.
Peel and devein the shrimp and slice in half lengthwise.

Slice the hard rolls in half, spread with lemon-garlic mayonnaise. Slice the filet into 4 pieces and
divide between sandwiches. Top with shrimp, a slice of grilled tomato and a small amount of the
shredded lettuce.

Lump Crab Cake and Fried Green Tomato on a Biscuit

{ Serves 4 }

1 red bell pepper
½ cup mayonnaise, divided
8 saltine crackers, crumbled fine
2 teaspoons Old Bay seasoning
8 ounces lump crabmeat
Canola oil, for frying
1 teaspoon unsalted butter
½ cup all-purpose flour
¼ cup cornmeal
¼ teaspoon cayenne pepper
½ teaspoon garlic powder
Kosher salt and freshly ground pepper
½ cup buttermilk
1 green tomato, sliced ¼-inch thick
4 3-inch biscuits

~

Char the red pepper over high flame until blackened, about 2 minutes per side. Place in a small bowl and cover with plastic wrap until cool enough to handle. Slide the charred skin from the pepper and remove the core, seeds and ribs and discard. In a blender, purée the roasted pepper with ¼ cup mayonnaise, ¼ teaspoon salt and pinch of black pepper until smooth. Remove from blender and set aside.

In a small bowl, combine saltine crumbs with Old Bay and mix well. Stir in mayonnaise and gently fold in crab. Divide and gently form into 4 3-inch round cakes. Refrigerate to firm, about 30 minutes.

Heat an 8-inch skillet over medium heat. Add 1 teaspoon oil and 1 teaspoon butter and heat and swirl until foam subsides. Cook crab cakes for 3 minutes per side or until lightly browned. Drain on paper towels and keep warm until ready to serve. Reserve pan for later use.

Mix flour, cornmeal, cayenne, garlic powder, salt and pepper in shallow plate. Place the buttermilk in a shallow bowl. Wipe the skillet and fill with ½ inch of canola oil. Heat over medium heat until a drop of flour sizzles. One by one, dip the tomato slices into the buttermilk, dredge in the flour mixture and then place in the oil to fry. Fry until golden brown, about 3 minutes per side. Drain on a paper towel lined plate and keep warm until serving.

To serve, slice the biscuits open, spread the red pepper mayonnaise on cut sides and layer with the fried green tomato and crab cake.

"I still really enjoy cooking Korean food, especially Korean barbeque."

Asian Slider Burger

{ Serves 4 }

½ pound ground beef or turkey
1 tablespoon finely chopped garlic
1 tablespoon finely chopped scallions
1 tablespoon soy sauce
¾ teaspoon toasted sesame seed oil
¼ cup mayonnaise
1 teaspoon wasabi (Japanese horseradish) paste, or more to taste
¼ cup pickled ginger
1 cup shredded iceberg lettuce
4 soft seeded rolls

~

In a small bowl, combine ground meat, garlic, scallions, soy and sesame oil. Mix with clean hands until combined. Divide mixture into 4 portions and pat into small burgers. Season on both sides with salt and pepper.

Heat a grill or grill pan over medium-high heat and cook the burgers, turning once, until cooked through, about 3 minutes per side. Remove to a paper towel lined plate to drain.

In a small bowl combine the mayonnaise and wasabi paste and mix well.

To make the burgers, spread wasabi mayonnaise on both sides of the bun, top with a burger, some pickled ginger and lettuce.

Ahn may have grown up eating Korean food, but these days his favorite guilty pleasure is foie gras and drinking champagne.

Mini Oyster and Crawfish Po' Boy

{ Serves 4 }

¼ cup finely chopped red onion (about ¼ small onion)
1 Roma tomato, diced
1 finely diced dill pickle spear or 2 tablespoons dill relish
1 lemon, juiced
⅓ cup mayonnaise
Kosher salt and freshly ground pepper
1 cup flour
½ cup cornmeal
1 teaspoon cayenne pepper
½ teaspoon onion powder
½ teaspoon garlic powder
Canola oil for frying
1 cup buttermilk
8 shucked fresh oysters
12 pieces of cooked crawfish tail meat
3 leaves Romaine lettuce
4 mini baguettes

~

In a small bowl, mix the onion, tomato, dill pickle, lemon juice and mayonnaise. Season with salt and pepper to taste and set aside to let the flavors develop.

Mix flour, cornmeal, cayenne, onion powder, garlic powder, ½ teaspoon each salt and pepper in shallow plate. Place the buttermilk in a shallow bowl. Heat an 8-inch skillet with ½ inch of canola oil and heat over medium-high heat to 350°.

Place the oysters and crawfish in the buttermilk. One by one, remove from the buttermilk, dredge in the flour mixture then dip again in the buttermilk and once again in the flour mixture. Repeat until all oysters are cooking. Place the double breaded oysters in the fry oil and repeat the process with the crawfish tails. Fry until golden brown, turning as needed, about 3 minutes. Remove with a slotted spoon to a paper towel lined plate and season with salt and pepper.

To serve, split each baguette from the top down, lengthwise, to create a bun. Open the bun and spread with the mayonnaise mixture, top with shredded lettuce and then divide the fried oysters and crawfish between the buns. Serve hot.

Italian Mini

{ Serves 4 }

1 cup arugula
1 teaspoon mashed garlic
2 tablespoons toasted pine nuts
2 tablespoons grated parmesan cheese
8 fresh basil leaves
1 roasted red bell pepper, cored, seeds and skin removed
⅓ cup extra virgin olive oil, additional for brushing grill
Kosher salt and fresh ground pepper
4 small wedges focaccia
4 ounces thinly sliced prosciutto
4 ounces sliced sopressata
4 ounces thinly sliced fresh mozzarella
8 pepperoncini peppers

~

Place the arugula, garlic, pine nuts, parmesan, basil and roasted pepper in a blender container. With the blender running, drizzle in the olive oil and blend until smooth. Season to taste with salt and pepper.

Heat a grill pan over medium-high heat. Brush with oil. Slice the focaccia wedges in half, widthwise to make 2 thin wedges. Spread the cut halves with the pesto, put back together and grill until nicely toasted, about 2 minutes per side.

Open the bread and layer the prosciutto, sopressata and fresh mozzarella on the bottom wedge, cover with the top and serve with pepperoncini peppers.

WHAT TO DRINK

Delightful little sandwiches with playful sliders deserve just the right beer for the occasion. Be sure to select a more refreshing, lighter style to allow for versatility across the international flavors of this fun instant party food.

was born into the restaurant industry. His parents owned a restaurant in Gettysburg, Pennsylvania. "I grew up working in the restaurant. So did all my brothers—becoming a chef was a natural progression." Cooking is a family affair—Ahn's father's mother taught Ahn's mom to cook and she then taught him. "My mom's egg rolls are on my menu today— I think the first thing I learned how to cook was a Korean dumpling from my mom."

What's something people would be surprised to find out about you?
I love games. My wife and I play backgammon all the time.

What movies could you watch over and over?
Spaceballs, History of the World, Part 1 and *Fletch*.

If you could have a theme song playing every time you walk into the kitchen, what would it be?
"Into the Mystic" by Van Morrison.

Where would you like to visit that you've never been before?
I would love to visit the Galapagos Islands. That would be a cool place to see.

What food do you find most difficult to work with?
There is a fish I hate to cook called wahoo. It gets dry so quick— on the turn of a dime.

What are your hobbies?
I love to play golf and to scuba dive.

What's your favorite drink?
It used to be bourbon but now it's champagne. It goes with whatever you are eating.

Where did you go to school?
The Culinary Institute of America in Hyde Park, NY. I went right out of high school.

219

JOSHUA PERKINS

Sunday Dinner with Friends

Heirloom Tomato Salad with Aged Goat Cheese

Spring Pea and Lemon Risotto

Whole Roasted Sea Bass with Artichokes Barigoule

Roast Organic Chicken with Grilled Vegetables and Potato Puree

Spanish Chocolate Tart

Heirloom Tomato Salad with Aged Goat Cheese

{ Serves 6 }

2 large vine ripe tomatoes, cored and cut into wedges
¼ cup unseasoned rice vinegar
1 teaspoon kosher salt
1 teaspoon granulated sugar
8 large heirloom tomatoes, assorted colors and sizes
8 fresh basil leaves, divided
4 ounces aged goat cheese, crumbled

~

Purée the vine ripe tomatoes in a blender and transfer to a medium saucepan. Heat over medium heat, stirring occasionally, until heated through and barely starting to simmer. Remove from heat. Line a strainer with a coffee filter and place over a bowl. Pour warm tomato puree into the filter and let the juices run into the bowl below. Do not press on the pulp-let the juice naturally drip through. This will take a few hours. Discard the pulp and save the tomato liquid (referred to as tomato water).

In a large mixing bowl, combine 1 cup of tomato water with the rice vinegar, salt and sugar. Stir to combine, taste and adjust seasoning, as needed, with salt and sugar to achieve a balance of sweet and salty flavor. If you have leftover tomato water, you can freeze for later use.

Rinse the heirloom tomatoes, remove the core and cut into wedges. Combine the tomato wedges with the tomato vinaigrette and 2 torn basil leaves; let marinate for at least 1 hour. Place the tomatoes on a large platter, sprinkle with the crumbled goat cheese, drizzle with the tomato juices, and garnish with the remaining 6 basil leaves.

Spring Pea and Lemon Risotto

{ Serves 6 }

2½ pounds fresh English peas in the pods (about 1 cup peas)
6 cups water
Kosher salt
3 tablespoons unsalted butter, divided
2 tablespoons extra virgin olive oil, divided
1 lemon
1 clove garlic, minced
2 shallots, minced
3 cups Carnaroli or Vialone Nano rice (high quality Arborio rice)
½ cup freshly grated Parmigiano-Reggiano cheese
Kosher salt and freshly ground white pepper
Additional freshly grated Parmigiano-Reggiano for serving

~

Shell the peas, reserving the pods. Place the pods in a medium pot with 6 cups of lightly salted water. Bring to a boil over high heat, reduce the heat to medium-low, and simmer, uncovered, for an hour. Strain the broth into a medium pot, pressing on the pods. Discard the pods. Keep the broth warm over medium heat.

Melt 1 tablespoon butter and 1 tablespoon oil in a heavy, medium-sized Dutch oven over medium-low heat. Add the peas and ½ cup of the broth. Cover and cook until the peas are tender, about 5 minutes. Strain the peas and reserve for later use.

In the now empty same pot, increase the heat to medium-high, add remaining 1 tablespoon oil, the garlic and shallots and cook, stirring until they begin to sweat, but not color, about 5 minutes. Add the rice and stir to coat well. Add ¾ cup warm pea broth and cook, stirring constantly, until most of the broth has been absorbed. Add more broth a little at a time and continue cooking, stirring and adding broth as needed, until the rice is tender but firm to the bite, about 18 minutes. Remove from the heat and stir in just enough broth so that the rice is loose but not watery, about ½ cup. Stir in the remaining 2 tablespoons butter, zest of half the lemon and Parmigiano-Reggiano and season with salt and white pepper to taste. Cover and allow to rest for a few minutes. Sprinkle with remaining lemon zest. Serve with an additional fresh grating of Parmigiano-Reggiano.

* If fresh peas are not available, use frozen petit peas and vegetable stock in place of the pea stock.

"I think it is just as important to feel and understand the roots of a dish as it is to know how to cook it. It gives you a deeper level of passion for the process."

Whole Roasted Sea Bass with Artichokes Barigoule

{ Serves 4 }

7 lemons
1 whole sea bass, head on (about 3 pounds), cleaned and gutted
1 tablespoon kosher salt
2 teaspoons freshly ground white pepper
3 tablespoons finely chopped fresh rosemary
3 tablespoons finely chopped fresh thyme
3 tablespoons olive oil, divided
8 fresh baby artichokes (or 1 14-ounce can artichoke hearts)
1 medium onion, diced
2 cloves garlic, finely chopped
1 small carrot, peeled and diced
2 tablespoons finely chopped fresh parsley, more for garnish
1 tablespoon chiffonade of fresh basil, more for garnish
1 fresh bay leaf
½ cup dry white wine
2 tablespoons unsalted butter
Kosher salt and freshly ground white pepper

~

Preheat oven to 425°. Thinly slice 4 of the lemons and arrange half of the lemon slices on the bottom of a non-reactive (such as stainless steel or a glass Pyrex baking dish) roasting pan. Season the fish inside and out with salt, white pepper, rosemary and thyme. Place the seasoned fish on top of the lemon slices and cover the fish with the remaining lemon slices. Drizzle with 1 tablespoon of the olive oil. Bake fish until it is cooked through at the thickest part, about 30 minutes.

While the fish is cooking, prepare the baby artichokes. Cut the artichoke stems to 1½ inches. Cut off the top ¼-inch of the artichoke and remove the outer two or three tough leaves. Peel the stem and bottom of the artichoke, cut in half and remove the center choke with a spoon; place in a bowl of ice water with juice of 1 lemon.

Heat a heavy-bottom Dutch oven over medium heat, add the remaining 2 tablespoons olive oil to cover bottom of pan. Add the onion, garlic and carrot. Slowly cook until golden brown, 5-7 minutes. Place the prepared artichokes on top of the onion-carrot mixture in a single layer. Add the parsley, basil and bay leaf. Season with salt and pepper. Add the wine and enough water to just cover the artichokes. If using fresh artichoke hearts, cover and cook over medium heat until tender, about 15 minutes (if using canned artichokes, simply cook until heated through, about 5 minutes). Uncover, increase the temperature, and continue to cook until the liquid is reduced. Remove the bay leaf and discard; remove the artichoke hearts and reserve. Whisk in the butter and season with salt and pepper to taste.

To serve, remove lemons from the fish and discard. Place the fish in the center of a warm platter, surround with the artichokes in the butter sauce and drizzle with the pan juices. Serve immediately garnished with the remaining 2 fresh lemons and herbs.

Roast Organic Chicken with Grilled Vegetables and Potato Puree

{ Serves 4 }

2 whole organic chickens
3 large cloves of garlic, peeled
5 sprigs fresh rosemary
5 sprigs fresh thyme
2 shallots, peeled and quartered
2 large lemons, cut in half
6 medium Yukon gold potatoes, peeled and quartered
4 tablespoons unsalted butter, in pieces
¾ cup heavy cream

1 bunch asparagus, tough ends removed
1 red bell pepper cut in half, stem and seeds removed
1 yellow pepper cut in half, stem and seeds removed
1 eggplant, sliced lengthwise, ¼-inch thick
1 zucchini, sliced lengthwise, ¼-inch thick
3 tablespoons olive oil
Kosher salt
Black pepper

~

Preheat oven to 400°. Adjust oven racks to accommodate the chicken on center rack.

Rub the chickens inside and out with salt and black pepper. Stuff the inside of the chickens with the garlic, rosemary, thyme, shallots and lemons. Place the chickens, breast side up, in a shallow heavy roasting pan, making sure the birds are not touching. Place the pan in the oven, roast for 20 minutes, reduce the heat to 350° and continue roasting for another 30 minutes. A thermometer in the thigh will reach 170° and the juices will run clear. Remove from oven and let rest for 15 minutes before carving. Serve on warm platter.

Place peeled and quartered potatoes in a large pot and cover with cold water, bring to a boil over high heat and simmer, uncovered, for about 30 minutes or until fork tender. Drain the potatoes, return to the pot to dry out any remaining moisture and mash with a potato masher, or pass through a food mill. While the potatoes are still hot add the butter and heavy cream. Season with salt and pepper to taste. Beat until smooth. Serve on warm platter.

Preheat grill or grill pan to medium heat. Place the asparagus, peppers, eggplant and zucchini in a large mixing bowl, drizzle with the olive oil and toss to coat. Season with salt and pepper. Place the vegetables in a single layer on the preheated grill. Slightly char the vegetables on each side, until they are cooked through. Remove from grill to a warm platter.

Spanish Chocolate Tart

{ Serves 8 }

DOUGH
2 cups all-purpose flour
2 tablespoons almond flour
Pinch of baking powder
6 tablespoons unsalted butter
½ cup granulated sugar
1 large egg yolk
1 large egg
3 tablespoons ice water

FILLING
16 tablespoons (2 sticks) unsalted butter
¾ cup granulated sugar
5 large eggs, room temperature
14 ounces bittersweet chocolate, melted
    and kept slightly warm

~

Preheat oven to 350°. In a small bowl combine the flour, almond flour and baking powder, whisk to combine. In the bowl of a stand mixer fitted with the paddle, cream the butter and gradually add the sugar, egg yolk and egg, scraping down the sides of the bowl as needed. Turn the mixer to low, add the flour mixture, mixing until just combined. Drizzle in the ice water. The dough will look crumbly but should hold together when squeezed in the palm of your hand. Turn the dough out onto plastic wrap and form into a disk. Cover and let rest in the refrigerator for an hour.

Spray a 10-inch springform pan with cooking spray and set on a baking sheet lined with parchment paper. Roll the dough ¼-inch thick and in a circle slightly larger than the pan. Lay the dough over the pan and press the dough into the corners and halfway up the sides of the pan. Let rest in the refrigerator for 30 minutes. Prick the dough with a fork, line with parchment or foil and fill with pie weights or dried beans. Bake the crust for 5 minutes, remove the weights and parchment or foil and continue baking for another 3-5 minutes, just until starting to brown. (This procedure is called blind baking.) Remove from oven to cool and reduce heat of oven to 300°.

FILLING In a bowl of a stand mixer cream the butter and the sugar. Mix in the eggs one at a time, scraping down sides of the bowl between each addition. The mixture will look a little curdled, not emulsified and smooth. Slowly mix in the warm, melted chocolate. Fill the tart shell level with the sides. Place in the oven and bake for 25-30 minutes until just beginning to set and the center barely shakes. Cool on a rack for 30 minutes and then completely cool in the refrigerator before serving.

WHAT TO DRINK

Consider Sauvignon Blanc for this light, spring menu. The wine's grassy and citrus character exudes freshness. There should be no problem with this wine carrying through until dessert. With the tart's spicy chocolate flavors enjoy a demi-sec champagne.

JOSHUA PERKINS

became interested in cooking in fourth grade. As a child growing up in Memphis, Perkins wanted to be a doctor until he was faced with a geography project and learned how to prepare his very first dish: jambalaya. Perkins' most memorable moment was his first day in Italy working at a Michelin star restaurant. "It was one of those experiences you always wanted to have growing up, but only halfway believed you actually would."

What movies could you watch over and over?
Mad Dog Time, Big Night, Lock, Stock and Two Smoking Barrels.

What's your most used quote in the kitchen?
"It is what it is."

What music never gets old to you?
Anything by Thievery Corporation and St. Germain.

Name a famous person you've cooked for?
Mick Jagger.

Who has provided the most inspiration to you?
Eric Ripert, Marco Pierre White.

What's your favorite place to eat when you're not at your own restaurant?
Aria.

In high school, you were voted...
Most talkative.

What are you scared of?
Spiders and heights.

What are your favorite books?
White Heat by Marco Pierre White, *It's Not How Good You Are, It's How Good You Want To Be* by Paul Arden.

What's your favorite drink?
Guinness.

DAVID HARTSHORN

EINSTEIN'S

Picnic at the Park

Fusilli Pasta Salad

Portobello Mushroom Sandwich with Brie Cheese

Piedmont Park Potato Salad

Flank Steak Sandwich

Prosciutto Panini

Fusilli Pasta Salad

{ Serves 6 }

8 ounces dry fusilli or rotini pasta, cooked al denté and rinsed with cold water
½ cup finely diced yellow onion
¼ cup finely diced green bell pepper
¼ cup finely diced red bell pepper
10 leaves fresh basil, chiffonade
4 ounces feta cheese, crumbled
½ cup Champagne Vinaigrette
Kosher salt and freshly ground pepper

~

In a large mixing bowl combine the cooked pasta, onion, bell peppers, basil, and feta and toss gently. Pour the vinaigrette over the salad and toss again. If the salad seems dry add more vinaigrette. Season with salt and pepper and serve.

CHAMPAGNE VINAIGRETTE

{ Makes 7 ounces }

¼ cup champagne vinegar
⅛ cup Creole mustard
¾ teaspoon sugar
½ cup vegetable oil
Salt and freshly ground white pepper to taste

~

In the bowl of a food processor combine vinegar, mustard and sugar until combined. With the machine running slowly drizzle the oil into this mixture until all of the oil is incorporated and the mixture is emulsified. Season with salt and pepper to taste. You can store leftover vinaigrette in a tightly covered container in the refrigerator for 1 week.

Portobello Mushroom Sandwich with Brie Cheese

{ Serves 4 }

2 tablespoons olive oil
8 medium portobello mushroom caps
Kosher salt and freshly ground pepper
2 cups packed fresh spinach leaves, washed and stemmed (about 6 ounces)
¼ cup Champagne Vinaigrette (see previous page)
4 tablespoons Roasted Red Pepper Aioli
4 pieces of 5-inch square soft Focaccia bread, sliced lengthwise
8 ounces brie cheese, sliced into 8 slices
1 large red tomato, sliced into 8 slices
1 large yellow tomato, sliced into 8 slices

~

Preheat grill to 350° or a grill pan to medium-high heat. Brush both sides of mushrooms with olive oil and season with salt and pepper. Grill mushrooms approximately 5 minutes per side. Remove from heat and cover with foil to soften. When the mushrooms have cooled and softened, slice thin. In a medium sized bowl, toss the spinach with the champagne vinaigrette. For each sandwich, spread 1 tablespoon roasted red pepper aioli on bottom half of bread, top with mushrooms, 2 slices of brie, 2 slices of each red and yellow tomatoes, and ½ cup of spinach. Place tops on sandwiches.

This sandwich can be served as is or pressed like a panini. Preheat a panini press. (If you do not have a panini press you can use a George Foreman grill or a 10-inch grill pan over medium heat and wrap a brick or other heavy, flat object in foil and spray with cooking spray to use as a weight.) Place the sandwich on the panini press, close the top and cook until toasted 4-6 minutes. (If using pan and brick method cook for 2-3 minutes on each side or until the sandwich is toasted.)

ROASTED RED PEPPER AIOLI

1 egg yolk
½ teaspoon lemon juice
1 dash red Tabasco sauce
1 tablespoon white vinegar
½ cup extra virgin olive oil
2 teaspoons roasted garlic paste (see page 233)
1 slice roasted red pepper
Salt and pepper to taste

~

In a blender, on high speed, mix the egg yolk, lemon juice, and Tabasco until combined. While the blender is running, add the vinegar and then in a slow steady stream, drizzle in the olive oil to form a creamy emulsion. Add the roasted garlic, roasted red pepper and turn on medium speed to blend. Season the aioli with salt and pepper to taste.

Piedmont Park Potato Salad

{ Serves 8 }

3 teaspoons kosher salt, divided
1¾ pounds small red potatoes
½ pound asparagus, about 10 stalks, tough ends trimmed
½ cup finely diced sweet yellow onions
¼ cup toasted sliced almonds
2 tablespoons finely chopped tarragon
½ cup Champagne Vinaigrette (see page 230)
Kosher salt and freshly ground pepper

~

Fill a 6-quart stock pot three-fourths full with water. Stir in 2 teaspoons salt and the potatoes and bring to a boil. Once the potatoes have come to a boil reduce the heat to medium-low and simmer, uncovered for 20-25 minutes or until the potatoes are fork tender. Drain the potatoes and rinse with cold water to cool. Cut the potatoes in half or in quarters if they are not bite size.

Heat a 10-inch straight sided skillet with 5 cups of water and remaining 1 teaspoon of salt to a boil. Add the asparagus and bring back to a boil and cook the asparagus until it is crisp tender, about 45 minutes. Drain the asparagus and rinse with cold water to cool and cut into ¼-inch slices.

In a large mixing bowl combine potatoes, asparagus, onions, almonds, and tarragon and gently toss in champagne vinaigrette to coat. Taste; season with salt and pepper and serve.

"I remember staying up late at night making homemade root beer, cheese and yogurt with my father."

Flank Steak Sandwich

{ Serves 4 }

2 tablespoons olive oil, divided
Kosher salt and freshly ground pepper
1¼ pound flank steak
1 very thinly sliced large yellow onion
8 ounces cremini mushrooms, sliced
½ cup Roasted Garlic Aioli
4 mini 5-inch ciabatta (slipper bread), sliced to make a bun
6 ounces Gruyere cheese, cut into 8 slices

~

In a 10-inch heavy-bottom skillet heat 1 tablespoon olive oil over medium-high heat. Slice the flank steak across the grain and on the bias in very thin slices. Season the sliced flank steak with salt and pepper. Cook the steak for 2 minutes, turn and sear until just beginning to release juice, about another 2 minutes. Do not crowd the pan, work in batches if necessary. Remove the steak and the juice to a shallow plate and cover with foil. Reduce the heat to medium, add remaining tablespoon olive oil to pan and the onions. Cook the onions until translucent, approximately 5-6 minutes. Increase the heat to medium-high and add the mushrooms; cook another 3-4 minutes or until the mushrooms are tender. Season the onion and mushroom mixture with salt and pepper. Toss the steak in the pan with the mushrooms and onions to heat through, approximately 1 minute. Spread 1 tablespoon of aioli on both cut sides of each bun. Evenly divide the meat and vegetable mixture on the bottom halves of the ciabatta and top each sandwich with 2 slices of Gruyere. Then place the tops on the sandwiches and serve.

ROASTED GARLIC AIOLI

1 egg yolk
½ teaspoon lemon juice
1 dash red Tabasco sauce
2 teaspoons roasted Garlic Paste
1 tablespoon white vinegar
½ cup extra virgin olive oil
Salt and pepper to taste

~

In a blender, on high speed, mix the egg yolk, lemon juice, Tabasco and roasted garlic until combined. While the blender is running, add the vinegar and then in a slow steady stream, drizzle in the olive oil to form a creamy emulsion. Season the aioli with salt and pepper to taste.

GARLIC PASTE To quick roast garlic, place whole cloves in a small saucepan, add olive oil to cover. Cook over medium heat for 10 or 15 minutes until golden in color and very soft. Remove the garlic with a slotted spoon and mash with the flat side of a chef's knife to form a paste. Reserve the garlic oil for another use.

Prosciutto Panini

{ Serves 4 }

4 mini 5-inch ciabatta (slipper bread), sliced to make a bun
8 ounces prosciutto di Parma, sliced thin
8 ounces fresh mozzarella, cut into 8 slices
4 slices, about 2 whole, jarred roasted red peppers
1 large yellow tomato, sliced into 8 slices
¼ cup balsamic vinegar
2 tablespoons extra virgin olive oil

~

Preheat a panini press. (If you do not have a panini press you can use a 10-inch skillet over medium heat and wrap a brick in foil and spray with cooking spray to use as a weight.) For each sandwich, place 2 ounces prosciutto, 2 slices of mozzarella, 1 slice of roasted red pepper, and 2 slices of tomato on bottom half of ciabatta. Drizzle with 1 tablespoon of balsamic vinegar. Place top onto sandwich and brush top and bottom with olive oil. Place the sandwich into the panini press and cook until toasted 4-6 minutes. (If using pan and brick method cook for 2-3 minutes on each side or until the sandwich is toasted.)

Repeat cooking with the remaining 3 sandwiches and serve warm.

WHAT TO DRINK

When it comes to picnics, portability and ease of access come into play. Picnic wines should also be refreshing and thirst quenching. In recent years, New Zealand has blazed the path for screw cap wines and modern Sauvignon Blanc. Put these facts together, and you have your picnic choice already made. Alternatively, Aussie rosés made from Rhône varietals have shown promise and come conveniently sealed with screw caps.

DAVID HARTSHORN

is originally from New York and moved to Atlanta in 2000. His passion for cooking evolved in his early childhood when he used to cook with his parents. His mom's spaghetti sauce and tarragon chicken is currently on the menu at Einstein's. David's family had a large garden and fresh vegetables were always in surplus, which they would trade for meat from nearby farmers and local hunters.

What would you be if you weren't a chef?
A professional baseball player.

Who are some famous people you've cooked for?
Sharon Stone, Billy Joel, Bea Arthur, Keanu Reeves, Mary Stuart Masterson, Tony Danza, Kevin Spacey, Judd Hirsch, Bernadette Peters, Richard Dreyfuss and Bebe Neuwirth.

What other jobs have you had?
Stagehand for CBS-TV, the Metropolitan Opera House and Channel 13 in New York.

What movies could you watch over and over?
The Blues Brothers, 13th Warrior, Pride of The Yankees, and *Gladiator.*

If you could cook for anyone who would it be?
John Lennon or Paul McCartney.

What was the first dish you learned to cook?
I remember making chocolate mousse and asparagus with hollandaise sauce.

What's your most memorable moment in cooking?
I was working in New York doing the catering for the *Saturday Night Live* cast and crew. One night, Blues Traveler was the musical guest and after the show they couldn't find a restaurant still serving. They called us at Blake's and ordered a bunch of pizzas and beer. When we delivered it to the set, they invited us to any show, anytime, anywhere.

235

SCOTT PEACOCK

Low Country Boil

Salad of Fresh Summer Tomatoes and Butter Beans

Garlic Mayonnaise

Frogmore Stew

Blackberry Cobbler

Homemade Vanilla Ice Cream

Salad of Fresh Summer Tomatoes and Butter Beans

{ Serves 4 }

1 cup fresh shelled butter beans
Kosher salt and freshly ground pepper
4 large ripe tomatoes, cut into
    ½-inch wedges
18 cherry tomatoes, halved

1 small bunch of fresh basil
Extra virgin olive oil
Garlic Mayonnaise

~

Fill a saucepan three-fourths full with water. Add 1 tablespoon salt and bring to a rolling boil. Add beans and cook (blanch) for 3 minutes, or just until tender. Drain the beans in a colander and "shock" in a salted ice bath to stop the cooking.

Put the tomatoes into a large mixing bowl. Season well with salt and pepper to taste. Tear the basil leaves into large pieces and add to the tomatoes. Add just enough olive oil to lightly coat the tomatoes and basil and gently toss to combine. Remove the butter beans from the ice bath, drain, and add to the tomato mixture. Gently toss. Taste carefully for seasoning and turn onto a serving platter. Drizzle generously with garlic mayonnaise that has been thinned with a little hot water. Serve immediately passed with additional garlic mayonnaise on the side.

Garlic Mayonnaise

{ Makes 2 cups }

1 tablespoon cider vinegar
1 tablespoon freshly squeezed lemon juice
1 teaspoon sea salt
1 teaspoon dry mustard
2 large egg yolks
1½ cups vegetable oil, peanut oil, light olive oil, or a combination
3 tablespoons boiling water
2 large or 3 small cloves of garlic, rubbed into a paste with a pinch of sea salt

~

Combine vinegar, lemon juice, salt and dry mustard in a non-reactive bowl and whisk until the salt and mustard are dissolved. Add the egg yolks and beat until smooth. Add the oil, drop by drop first, and then in a slow steady stream, whisking constantly until all the oil has been incorporated and you have a very thick emulsion.

Pour the boiling water over the garlic paste and let stand for 1 minute. If there are any chunks, press through a sieve to remove. Whisk the garlic paste and water mixture into the finished mayonnaise until desired consistency and flavor. Thin to desired consistency with additional hot water.

Frogmore Stew

{ Serves 6 to 8 }

1½ pounds spicy smoked sausage
2 bell peppers
2 teaspoons vegetable oil
8 cups chicken stock
3 bay leaves
1 teaspoon dried thyme
18 small new potatoes, halved
2 medium onions, peeled and sliced lengthwise into ⅓-inch wedges
3 ears of corn, shucks and silks removed, cut into 4 pieces each
1 large tomato, peeled and seeded, cut into ½-inch pieces
Salt and freshly ground pepper
36 large fresh shrimp, head-on if available
1 tablespoon chopped fresh parsley

Preheat oven to 425°.

Place sausage in a large roasting pan. Rub the peppers with oil, and put them in the same pan. Roast in the preheated oven until the sausage is browned and cooked through, and the peppers begin to blister, about 20 minutes. Turn both the sausage and the peppers occasionally to ensure even cooking. Remove from the oven, and set aside until cool enough to handle. Bias cut the sausage into ½-inch pieces, and cut the peppers into ½-inch chunks.

Pour the chicken stock into a large non-reactive Dutch oven or heavy pot, and bring to a boil. Lower the heat to a simmer and add the bay leaves, thyme, potatoes and onions and cook, partially covered, for 10 minutes. Add the sausage, bell pepper, corn and tomato, and simmer, uncovered, until the potatoes and corn are cooked through, about 10 minutes. Taste and adjust seasoning with salt and pepper as needed. It should be highly flavored. Add the shrimp, and cook only until they are cooked through, 3-5 minutes. Remove from the heat, and sprinkle the parsley on top. Divide the shrimp, sausage, and vegetables between heated soup plates, ladle broth over all and serve.

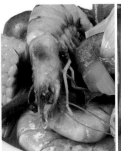

Blackberry Cobbler

{ Serves 6 }

1 recipe Pastry Dough
8 cups fresh blackberries
¾ cup granulated sugar
1 tablespoon all-purpose flour
¼ teaspoon salt
½ teaspoon fresh grated nutmeg
4 tablespoons (½ stick) unsalted butter, thinly sliced, divided
½ cup crushed sugar cubes
Homemade Vanilla Ice Cream

~

Preheat oven to 425°.

Divide the dough in half. Roll half of the dough to ⅛-inch thickness. Line a 2-quart, 2-inch deep baking dish with the dough. Trim the edges as needed, leaving ½-inch of pastry hanging over the rim of the dish. Cut any trimmings of pastry into 1-inch pieces and reserve.

Fill the pastry lined dish with the blackberries. Tuck any pieces of reserved dough in among the blackberries. With a whisk, mix the sugar, flour, salt, and nutmeg in a small bowl and sprinkle over the berries. Dot 3 tablespoons of the thinly sliced butter over the top. Refrigerate the dish while you roll out the top dough. Roll the remaining dough to a ⅛-inch thickness to top the cobbler. Trim the dough as needed, and add the trimmings and small pieces to the berries. Moisten the rim of the dough in the baking dish with a little cold water, and lay the top dough over. Gently press the edges together to seal, then fold the edge over inside the rim of the baking dish. With a sharp knife, cut a few 1-inch slits in the top dough to allow steam to escape. Sprinkle the crushed sugar cubes over the top, and dot with the remaining butter. Bake in the preheated oven for 20 minutes. Reduce heat to 375° and bake an additional 30-45 minutes, until the crust is a deep golden brown and the filling begins to bubble through the slits. Cool the cobbler on a rack until it is warm, and serve with homemade vanilla ice cream.

3 cups unbleached all-purpose flour
1½ teaspoons kosher salt
1 teaspoon granulated sugar
16 tablespoons (2 sticks) unsalted butter, cut into ½-inch pieces, and frozen 10 minutes
2 tablespoons lard, cut into ½-inch pieces, and frozen 10 minutes
8-12 tablespoons ice water

~

Put the flour, salt, and sugar on a large cutting board, and mix them with your fingers to blend. Put the frozen butter and lard on top of the flour mixture, and use a large kitchen knife or pastry cutter to quickly cut the fats into the flour until the mixture resembles coarse meal with some butter and lard pieces still as large as ½-inch in diameter. Ideally, half of the fat should be cut finely into the flour and the other half left in larger chunks.

Working quickly, gather the flour-fat mixture into a mound, and using your fingers, draw a trench lengthwise through the center. Sprinkle 2 tablespoons of the ice water down the length of the trench, and with spread, upturned fingers, fluff the flour so that it absorbs the water. Re-draw the trench and continue incorporating the ice water by tablespoons in the same manner. After you have incorporated 8 tablespoons of the water, the dough should begin to clump together into large pieces. If there are any un-massed areas, sprinkle them lightly with droplets of water and mix as before.

Gather the dough into a mass with a pastry scraper, and, again working quickly, with the heel of your hand smear a hunk of dough roughly the size of an egg by pushing it away from you. Continue with pieces of dough until the entire mass has been processed this way (you'll do about 6 smears in all). When finished, gather all the dough together with a pastry scraper and repeat the process. Re-gather the dough, quickly shape it into a flat disk, and wrap it in a double thickness of plastic wrap, pressing firmly with the palm of your hand to flatten the wrapped dough further and bind it. Divide the dough in half and refrigerate for at least 2 hours or overnight before rolling and using.

"Before I could walk, I watched my mother and grandmother in the kitchen. Cooking has always seemed magical to me, and I have always loved to eat."

Homemade Vanilla Ice Cream

½ vanilla bean
2 cups milk
8 egg yolks
¾ cup granulated sugar
2 cups heavy whipping cream
¾ teaspoon salt
3 tablespoons vanilla extract

~

Split the vanilla bean lengthwise and, with the tip of a paring knife, scrape the inside of the bean to remove the seeds. Mix the vanilla bean seeds and pod with the milk in a heavy-bottom non-reactive saucepan. Heat over medium-high heat, stirring occasionally, until the mixture is almost at the boiling point. Remove from heat, cover and let sit for 20 minutes to allow the milk to infuse with the vanilla flavor.

Place the egg yolks in a large mixing bowl and whisk in the sugar to blend. Slowly whisk 1 cup of the hot milk into the egg and sugar mixture to temper the egg yolks, and then stir the tempered yolks into the remaining hot milk in the saucepan. Return the saucepan to the stove and cook over moderate heat, stirring constantly with a wooden spoon, until most of the air bubbles that begin to cover the surface have dissipated and the custard thickens enough to coat the back of the spoon. Do not allow the custard to simmer or boil.

Remove from heat, and stir in the heavy cream. Allow the custard to cool completely, stir in the salt and vanilla extract, cover and chill overnight. Remove the chilled custard from the refrigerator and strain through a fine mesh strainer. Freeze the custard in an ice cream freezer, following manufacturer's directions. Pack in an airtight container and freeze until firm, 3-4 hours.

WHAT TO DRINK

Summertime is the right time for low country boils. And when the temperature rises, grab a refreshing Pale Ale. Microbreweries in the U.S. produce achingly fresh and hoppy versions of this British classic that wet the whistle and invigorate the palate. The clean flavors with hop balance will make fast friends with the sausage and shrimp from the boil, and the focused fizz will keep you reaching into the cooler for more. Try Anchor Liberty Ale or Sierra Nevada for an intro to this style.

SCOTT PEACOCK

is originally from Hartford, Alabama and has been interested in cooking for as long as he can
remember—or as he would phrase it "as long as I've been eating." The biggest inspiration
to him throughout his career was his great friend and mentor, Edna Lewis. In 2003,
he partnered with this legendary Southern chef to write a cookbook entitled,
The Gift of Southern Cooking: Recipes and Revelations from Two Great American Cooks.
A former chef of two former governors, Peacock is now the executive
chef at Watershed restaurant in Decatur.

**If you could cook for anyone,
who would it be?**
Leontyne Price.

**Finish the sentence, "I wish
I could..."**
Spend seven years traveling
slowly around the world.

**What's your favorite
guilty pleasure?**
Ice cream. My favorite flavor
is coffee.

**What's your most memorable
moment?**
Swimming with wild dolphins
in the Gulf.

What's your favorite kitchen tool?
My nutmeg grater.

**What's the strangest situation
you've been in on the job site?**
Working with inmates at the
Governor's mansion. It was fun...
but strange.

**Who are some famous people
you've cooked for?**
Oprah, Bill Clinton and
Jane Fonda.

What other jobs have you had?
In college I was a gas station
attendant.

**What was the first dish you
learned to cook?**
Oatmeal.

RAY BARATA

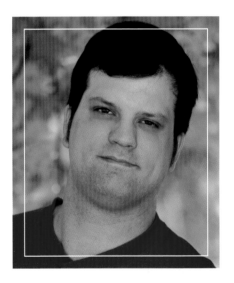

Meet the Neighbors
—

Southwestern Chicken Soup

Tomato Salad with Fresh Mozzarella and Lemon Vinaigrette

Shrimp Skewers with Cucumber and Red Onion Salad
and Scallion Vinaigrette

**Citrus Marinated Swordfish with Black Bean and Corn Relish
and a Duo of Chipotle and Cilantro Creams**

**Grilled Ribeye Steaks with Creamy Bleu Cheese Sauce
and Roasted Red Potatoes**

Southwestern Chicken Soup

{ Serves 4 to 6 }

6 6-inch diameter corn tortillas
2 tablespoons vegetable oil, more for tortillas
Kosher salt and freshly ground pepper
2 stalks celery, diced
1 cup diced white onion
1 large carrot, peeled and diced
1 teaspoon finely minced garlic
1 tablespoon finely chopped fresh thyme
1 bay leaf
¼ teaspoon ground cumin
8 cups chicken stock
1 pound cooked chicken, diced
¼ cup chopped fresh cilantro
¼ cup freshly squeezed lime juice
8 ounces cubed queso fresco or Monterey Jack cheese
1 avocado, peeled, pitted, and cubed

~

Heat oven to 400°. Brush 1 side of tortillas with oil; cut in half. Stack halves and cut crosswise into ¼-inch-wide strips. Spread strips on nonstick baking sheet. Season with salt and pepper. Bake until light golden, about 8 minutes. Set aside to cool.

Heat 2 tablespoons vegetable oil in a large pot over medium heat. Add the celery, onion, carrot, and garlic. Cook, stirring occasionally until the onions are translucent, 3-5 minutes. Add the thyme, bay leaf, cumin and chicken stock. Season with salt and pepper; bring to a boil then reduce heat to simmer. Cook until the vegetables are tender, about 10 minutes. Add the chicken and cook until heated through, 2-3 minutes. Stir in the cilantro and lime juice. Taste and adjust for seasoning with salt and pepper. Just before serving, divide the cheese among 4 to 6 bowls, and top with the baked tortilla strips. Ladle on the hot soup, garnish with avocado and serve immediately.

"Food always connects people. It's a great way to meet new people, and I love that."

Tomato Salad with Fresh Mozzarella and Lemon Vinaigrette

{ Serves 4 to 6 }

¼ cup lemon juice
2 tablespoons cider vinegar
2 teaspoons honey
3 tablespoons chopped fresh parsley
1½ teaspoons Dijon mustard
Kosher salt and freshly ground pepper
¼ cup extra virgin olive oil
1 head red leaf lettuce
1 pint grape tomatoes, halved
1 pint cherry tomatoes, halved
¾ cup Kalamata olives, pitted and diced
6 ounces fresh mozzarella, diced
½ cup shaved Parmigiano-Reggiano cheese

~

In the jar of a blender combine the lemon juice, cider vinegar, honey, parsley, mustard and a pinch of salt and pepper. Blend until smooth. With the blender on, remove the lid and slowly drizzle in the olive oil in a slow steady stream until mixture starts to thicken.

Line a platter with some of the outer leaves of the lettuce. Shred remaining lettuce and place on top of the leaves. In a large bowl, combine the tomatoes, olives, mozzarella and vinaigrette. Spoon tomato mixture on top of lettuce. Season with salt and pepper. Garnish with the shaved parmesan and serve immediately.

Shrimp Skewers with Cucumber and Red Onion Salad and Scallion Vinaigrette

{ Serves 4 }

1½ cups rice vinegar
2½ cups water
⅓ cup granulated sugar
1 teaspoon kosher salt
2 large English cucumbers, thinly sliced
1 small red onion, peeled and thinly sliced
12 6-inch bamboo skewers
½ cup chopped scallions
¼ cup water

¼ cup red wine vinegar
1 tablespoon Dijon mustard
1 tablespoon lemon juice
1 tablespoon honey
1 teaspoon kosher salt
1 cup olive oil
12 jumbo shrimp, peeled and deveined,
    tails intact
Kosher salt and freshly ground pepper

In a medium mixing bowl combine the rice vinegar, water, sugar and 1 teaspoon salt. Whisk until the sugar dissolves and fold in the cucumbers and red onion. Cover and let marinate in the refrigerator for at least 1 hour.

Place the bamboo skewers in water to soak, at least an hour.

Place the scallions, water, red wine vinegar, Dijon mustard, lemon juice, honey, and salt in the jar of a blender and purée until smooth. With the blender running, slowly drizzle in the olive oil. (Store in an airtight container in the refrigerator for up to 3 days.)

Heat a grill to medium-high. Skewer the shrimp lengthwise on the pre-soaked bamboo skewers, starting at the tail end; season with salt and pepper. Grill the shrimp until opaque, about 2 minutes per side. To serve, divide the cucumber salad between four plates, top each with three of the shrimp skewers and drizzle with scallion vinaigrette.

Citrus Swordfish with Black Bean and Corn Relish and a Duo of Chipotle and Cilantro Creams

{ Serves 4 }

½ yellow onion, finely diced
1 bunch fresh parsley, rinsed and chopped
2 cups freshly squeezed orange juice
½ cup lemon juice
¼ cup lime juice
¼ cup granulated sugar
4 6-ounce swordfish steaks
3 cups cooked black beans, rinsed & drained
1 cup cooked corn (fresh or frozen)
1 cup chopped scallions

1 finely diced red pepper
1 chipotle pepper in adobo sauce (canned)
½ cup plus 3 tablespoons water, divided
2 cups sour cream, divided
¾ cup heavy cream, divided
1 bunch fresh cilantro, rinsed well
⅛ teaspoon ground cumin
2 tablespoons olive oil, divided
2 cups arugula
Kosher salt and freshly ground pepper

~

In a medium bowl, combine the onion and parsley. Add the orange, lemon and lime juices and stir in sugar. Stir to combine. Reserve ¼ cup of the marinade and set aside. Place swordfish in a shallow container and pour remaining marinade over the fish. Cover with plastic wrap and refrigerate to marinate for 1 hour.

In a medium bowl combine the black beans, corn, scallions, red pepper and reserved ¼ cup marinade. Season to taste with salt and pepper. Set aside.

Wash and remove the seeds from the one chipotle in adobo. In a blender, purée the chipotle with 3 tablespoons water until smooth. Remove chipotle puree to a small bowl and fold in 1 cup of sour cream and ½ cup of heavy cream. Season with salt and pepper; set aside.

Clean the blender jar, purée the cilantro with the remaining ½ cup water until smooth. Remove cilantro puree to another small bowl and fold in the remaining 1 cup of sour cream, remaining ¼ cup heavy cream and cumin. Season with salt and pepper; set aside.

Heat grill to medium-high. Remove the swordfish from marinade and discard the used marinade. Brush the heated grill with 1 tablespoon oil and place fish on the grill. Grill for about 3-4 minutes, turn and repeat until the fish is almost cooked through. Remove from heat and let cool slightly.

To serve, toss the arugula with the remaining 1 tablespoon of oil in a medium bowl. Divide the arugula between 4 dinner plates. Top the arugula with 1 cup of black bean relish. Place swordfish on the plate and drizzle entire dish with 1 tablespoon each of the chipotle and cilantro cream sauces. Serve immediately.

Grilled Ribeye Steaks with Creamy Bleu Cheese Sauce and Roasted Red Potatoes

{ Serves 4 }

4 8- to 10-ounce ribeye steaks
Olive oil
Blackening seasoning

Kosher salt and freshly ground pepper
Creamy Bleu Cheese Sauce
Roasted Red Potatoes

~

Rub steaks lightly with olive oil and season with blackening seasoning and salt and pepper. Grill to desired doneness, 135° for rare. To serve, place potatoes in the center of the plate. Set the grilled steak atop the potatoes and top with bleu cheese sauce.

CREAMY BLEU CHEESE SAUCE

4 tablespoons unsalted butter
¼ cup all-purpose flour
1½ cups whole milk
¼ cup olive oil

¼ teaspoon salt
1 teaspoon freshly chopped parsley
½ teaspoon finely minced garlic
1 cup bleu cheese crumbles

~

Melt butter in medium-sized saucepan, whisk in flour and stir, over medium heat, until flour is cooked (3-4 minutes). Whisk in milk and olive oil and continue whisking until sauce begins to thicken. Add salt, parsley, garlic and bleu cheese. Stir until smooth. Keep warm until service.

ROASTED RED POTATOES

2 pounds red "new" potatoes
½ cup olive oil

½ teaspoon kosher or coarse sea salt
⅛ teaspoon white pepper

~

Quarter the red potatoes and toss them in a mixing bowl with the olive oil. Add salt and white pepper and mix well. Place on a rimmed baking sheet and bake at 350° for 20-25 minutes.

WHAT TO DRINK

When flavors are bold with a myriad of spices, there's no better pair than the complex and robust wine of France's Rhône Valley. Start out with one of the charming whites of the Northern Rhône based on Roussane, Viognier or Marsanne leading into the ribeye.

When the meat comes to the table, unleash an untamed red blend from the Southern Rhône like a Châteauneuf-du-Pape. With their tight tannins these wines are best when decanted.

RAY BARATA

is originally from New York. His family moved to South Georgia when he was young. Intrigued by cooking his whole life, he moved to Atlanta in 2000 to attend the Culinary Institute of Atlanta. Ray began his cooking career at Garrison's in Vinings as kitchen help and worked his way up the ladder to executive chef. With immediate family in Cuba, Barata's Cuban roots help him in developing his menu of flavorful dishes. Ray's favorite foods to cook are Ropa Vieja (shredded beef) and Cuban pork.

If you could cook for anyone, who would it be?
My grandmother. She was a huge influence in my mom's cooking.

What's your favorite guilty pleasure?
Waffle House at 2 a.m.

What food do you find most difficult to work with?
Sweet potatoes. I can't stand them.

If you could have a theme song playing every time you walk into the kitchen, what would it be?
"Eye of the Tiger" by Survivor.

What's the strangest food you've ever consumed?
True haggis in England.

What other jobs have you had?
A plumber's assistant, a construction worker, I worked in a feed factory, and I delivered pizza.

What movies could you watch over and over?
Scarface, Dumb and Dumber, Forrest Gump, and *The Godfather.*

What are your favorite vacation spots?
Las Vegas, Miami, and Spain.

DEAN DUPUIS

Not Your Average BBQ

Honey Barbecued Chicken Livers

Grilled Spice Crusted Tuna with BBQ Mushrooms and Shrimp

Barbecued Pulled Duck Sandwich with Pickled Green Tomatoes,
Watercress and Smoked Jalapeño-Honey Mustard

BBQ White Beans

Barbecued Potatoes au Gratin

South City Kitchen Homemade BBQ Sauce and Master BBQ Spice Rub

Honey Barbecued Chicken Livers

{ Serves 4 }

1 pound chicken livers, trimmed
2 tablespoons SCK Master BBQ Spice Rub, additional pinch for the glaze (page 261)
2 cups buttermilk
16 6-inch bamboo skewers
8 slices applewood smoked bacon, each slice cut in half
1 large Vidalia onion, cut into 8 wedges
Kosher salt and freshly ground pepper
¼ cup honey
1 tablespoon cider vinegar
Vegetable oil, for the grill

~

Place the livers in a large bowl and sprinkle with the spice rub. Pour the buttermilk over the livers, cover with plastic wrap, and refrigerate to marinate at least 4 hours or overnight.

Soak bamboo skewers in water for 30 minutes before using. Using two skewers, side by side, about ¼-inch apart, skewer chicken livers and onion wedges and wrap lengthwise with a piece of bacon, securing with skewers below the liver and above the onion. (Using two skewers will make it easier to turn on the grill.) Season with salt and pepper.

In a small bowl whisk together the honey, cider vinegar and a pinch of spice rub.

Heat an outdoor grill to high. Brush the heated grill with oil and place skewers on the grill, bacon side down. Brush the liver and onion with honey-vinegar mixture. Cook until bacon starts to brown, about 3 minutes. Turn skewers, brush again with honey-vinegar mixture and grill for another 3 minutes or until bacon starts to char and chicken livers are cooked to medium. Serve immediately.

Grilled Spice Crusted Tuna with BBQ Mushrooms and Shrimp

{ Serves 4 to 6 }

½ pound assorted mushrooms such as cremini, portobello, shiitake, and oyster
4 tablespoons canola oil, divided
South City Kitchen Homemade BBQ Sauce (page 260)
12 jumbo shrimp, peeled and deveined
1 lemon
4 5-ounce portions of number 1 grade tuna
2 tablespoons SCK Master Spice Rub (page 261)
Kosher salt and black pepper

~

Preheat grill with your favorite hardwood such as hickory or mesquite. If using a gas grill, use a smoker box with wood chips on the briquettes.

Slice the mushrooms into ½-inch slices. Place mushrooms in a small bowl and toss with 1 tablespoon canola oil. Season with salt and pepper. Add 3 tablespoons of the BBQ sauce and mix well. Set aside.

In a small bowl, toss the shrimp with 2 teaspoons canola oil, the juice from the lemon, 3 tablespoons of BBQ sauce, and salt and pepper. Set aside.

Rub all sides of the tuna with canola oil. Season with salt and pepper and coat all sides with the spice rub. Set aside.

Using a vegetable grill basket or aluminum foil with holes in it, place mushrooms on the grill and cook until golden brown, about 10 minutes. Remove and keep warm.

Grill shrimp, until curled and bright pink, about 4 minutes, turning to cook both sides. Remove and keep warm.

Grill tuna on all sides, about 1 minute per side for rare.

To serve, place sliced tuna in the center of the plate, top with BBQ mushrooms and surround with BBQ shrimp. Drizzle warm BBQ sauce around the plate.

"I like to make food that is fun and whimsical."

Barbecued Pulled Duck Sandwich with Pickled Green Tomatoes, Watercress and Smoked Jalapeño-Honey Mustard

{ Serves 4 to 6 }

½ cup dark molasses
¼ cup orange juice
2 tablespoons finely chopped garlic
¼ cup cider vinegar
2 tablespoons honey
½ teaspoon crushed red pepper
Kosher salt and black pepper
8 duck leg quarters
8 slices Texas toast
4 tablespoons unsalted butter, melted
1 bunch baby watercress
Pickled Green Tomatoes
Smoked Jalapeño-Honey Mustard

~

Preheat oven to 500°. Combine the dark molasses, orange juice and garlic in a small saucepan over low heat.

Meanwhile, combine the cider vinegar, honey and crushed red pepper in a medium bowl. Season with salt and pepper; set aside. Season the duck legs liberally with salt and pepper. Heat a large heavy-bottom ovenproof skillet over medium-high heat. Add the duck quarters and sear both sides until brown and some of the fat has rendered, about 3 minutes per side. (Pour off the fat and reserve for another use.) Brush the quarters with glaze and turn the quarters skin side down; transfer to the oven and bake for 15 minutes.

Reduce the temperature to 275°. Brush glaze over quarters again and remove glaze from the heat. Continue roasting, brushing with glaze every 20 minutes or so, until the duck is falling off the bone and the skin is a deep, dark caramelized color, about 1½ hours.

Remove the duck to a plate to cool slightly. Remove and discard the skin; shred the duck with your fingers. Place shredded duck in a medium glass bowl and toss with the reserved honey-cider vinegar mixture. Taste and adjust for seasoning with salt and pepper; set aside.

Butter both sides of the Texas toast with the melted butter. Heat a medium non-stick skillet over medium heat. Add the toast and cook until golden brown on both sides. Spoon shredded duck onto the buttered Texas toast. Add green tomatoes, a teaspoon or more of the jalapeño-honey mustard, and some baby watercress. Top with the other half of the Texas toast and enjoy.

PICKLED GREEN TOMATOES

{ Makes 1 quart }

These easy refrigerator pickles are best made at least 12 hours ahead. Since they are not processed in a canning kettle, they must be kept in the refrigerator.

4 medium to large green tomatoes, sliced ⅛-inch thick
¼ cup water
3 tablespoons granulated sugar
2 tablespoons unseasoned rice wine vinegar
1½ teaspoons kosher salt
½ whole clove
¼ teaspoon mustard seeds
¼ teaspoon whole black peppercorns
¼ teaspoon finely minced fresh ginger

~

Place the tomatoes in a large non-reactive glass or stainless steel bowl; set aside.

Combine the water, sugar, vinegar, salt, clove, mustard seeds, peppercorns, and ginger in a small non-reactive saucepan. Bring to a boil. Pour the hot liquid over the sliced green tomatoes. Let cool then cover with plastic wrap. Store the quick pickled tomatoes in an airtight container in the refrigerator for up to 1 week.

SMOKED JALAPEÑO-HONEY MUSTARD

{ Makes 2½ cups }

1 tablespoon canned chipotle pepper in adobo
1 cup mayonnaise, preferably Duke's
1 cup Creole mustard
½ cup honey
1 teaspoon lemon juice
½ teaspoon finely chopped fresh garlic
Kosher salt and freshly ground pepper to taste

~

Combine the chipotle, mayonnaise, mustard, honey, lemon juice and garlic in the jar of a blender and mix on high speed until combined. Store the honey mustard in an airtight container in the refrigerator for up to 3 weeks.

BBQ White Beans

{ Serves 12 }

2 cups dried great Northern beans
4 quarts water, more for cooking the beans
10 slices applewood smoked bacon, diced
1½ cups finely chopped Vidalia onions
½ cup finely chopped carrots
1 tablespoon finely chopped garlic
1 cup brown sugar, firmly packed
1 cup South City Kitchen Homemade BBQ Sauce (page 260)
2 tablespoons molasses
Pinch crushed red pepper flakes
Pinch allspice
1 tablespoon kosher salt
1 tablespoon black pepper

~

Fill a heavy-bottom Dutch oven with 4 quarts of warm water. Place beans in this water and soak overnight. Pour soaked beans into a colander to drain.

Heat a large heavy-bottom Dutch oven over medium-low heat. Add the bacon and cook until soft and the fat has rendered, about 8 minutes. Increase the heat to medium-high and add the onions, carrots and garlic and sauté until soft, about 5 minutes; season with salt and black pepper. Add the drained, soaked beans, brown sugar, BBQ sauce, molasses, pepper flakes and allspice and stir to combine. Add enough water to cover the beans by 2 inches. Bring to a boil then reduce the heat to simmer. Cook until the beans are tender and the mixture is thick, 2½-3½ hours. Taste and adjust for seasoning with salt and pepper. Serve immediately.

Barbecued Potatoes au Gratin

{ Serves 8 }

4 tablespoons unsalted butter, more for the baking dish
1 large Vidalia onion, thinly sliced
½ teaspoon sugar
Pinch kosher salt and black pepper
6 medium Yukon gold potatoes
1 tablespoon kosher salt
½ teaspoon black pepper
3 cups heavy cream
3 large cloves finely chopped garlic
Pinch freshly grated nutmeg
½ cup South City Kitchen Homemade BBQ Sauce (Page 260)
1½ cups grated Asiago cheese

~

Melt butter in a small heavy-bottom saucepan. Add onion with ½ teaspoon of sugar, and a pinch of kosher salt and black pepper. Cook the onions, stirring occasionally, until caramelized and dark brown, about 30 minutes.

Preheat oven to 325°. Fill a large bowl with cold water. Peel and slice the Yukon gold potatoes into ¼-inch rounds. Place in cold water as you slice. (This will keep the potatoes from browning.)

Drain the potatoes well and place in a medium heavy-bottom saucepan. Pour the heavy cream over the potatoes. Add 1 tablespoon salt and ½ teaspoon pepper to the cream mixture. Cook over low heat for about 8-10 minutes.

Using a slotted spoon remove the potatoes from the cream. Reserve the cream. Layer the potatoes and caramelized onions in an 8- x 10-inch baking dish. Combine the reserved heavy cream, BBQ sauce, garlic and hefty pinch of nutmeg. Stir to combine and season with kosher salt and black pepper to taste. Pour BBQ cream mixture over potatoes to cover. Top with the 1½ cups of shredded Asiago cheese.

Bake until bubbly and golden brown, 30-45 minutes. Remove from the oven and let this rest for 5 minutes before serving.

"I'd love to travel to Spain. It's a staging ground for food trends that I'd love to experience."

South City Kitchen Homemade BBQ Sauce

{ Makes 6½ cups }

2 tablespoons canola oil
1 cup finely chopped onion (about 1 onion)
2 tablespoons finely chopped garlic
2 cups cider vinegar
2 cups tomato juice
1 cup maple syrup
⅔ cup granulated sugar
½ cup light brown sugar, firmly packed
½ cup ketchup
¼ cup lemon juice
¼ cup dark molasses
1 tablespoon mustard powder
Kosher salt and freshly ground pepper

~

Heat the oil in a large heavy-bottom saucepan over medium-high heat. Add the onion and cook until translucent, 3-5 minutes. Add garlic and cook until fragrant, about 1 minute. Add vinegar, tomato juice, maple syrup, granulated sugar, brown sugar, ketchup, lemon juice, molasses and mustard powder. Season with salt and pepper. Reduce the heat to a simmer and cook until well-flavored and thick, about 1 hour. Taste and adjust for seasoning with salt and pepper. (For a thicker sauce, continue to cook to desired consistency.)

"My best friend, Chip, has been the biggest inspiration to my career. He hired me to work at a four-diamond restaurant in South Carolina, and really helped me develop as a chef."

South City Kitchen Master BBQ Spice Rub

{ Makes 2½ cups }

1 cup paprika
¼ cup smoked paprika
¼ cup cumin
¼ cup kosher salt
¼ cup black pepper
¼ cup granulated sugar
¼ cup brown sugar, firmly packed
2 tablespoons garlic powder
1 teaspoon ground cinnamon
1 teaspoon ground cloves

~

Combine the paprika, smoked paprika, cumin, salt, pepper, sugar, brown sugar, garlic powder, cinnamon and cloves in a medium bowl and stir to combine. Store the spice rub in an airtight container for up to 1 month.

WHAT TO DRINK

Any time barbecue is involved, go straight for a California Zinfandel. The wine's vibrant, brambly fruit character anchored by its molasses texture and long finish give the barbecue an equal dance partner.

DEAN DUPUIS

SOUTH CITY KITCHEN
~
VININGS

Southern Seafood Feast

Cornmeal Crusted Oysters with Fennel-Grapefruit Salad
and Maple-Mustard Sauce

Shrimp Bisque with Bacon Cheddar Crumbs

Heirloom Tomato and Seared Scallop Salad

Crispy Grouper with Arugula-Peach Salad
and Bourbon-Brown Sugar Vinaigrette

Butterscotch Pudding with Candied Orange Peel
and Maple Pecan Sandies

Cornmeal Crusted Oysters with Fennel-Grapefruit Salad and Maple-Mustard Sauce

{ Serves 4 }

20 fresh oysters
2 cups buttermilk
2 cups cornmeal
1 pinch cayenne pepper
1½ teaspoons garlic powder
2 teaspoons salt
2 teaspoons freshly ground pepper
Canola oil (for frying)
Fennel-Grapefruit Salad
Maple-Mustard Sauce

~

Place the oysters in a strainer and rinse with cold water. Drain on paper towels and place in a medium bowl. Add buttermilk and gently fold with a large spoon to combine.

In a shallow plate, combine the cornmeal with the cayenne, garlic powder, salt and pepper.

Heat a cast iron Dutch oven over medium-high heat. Add enough canola oil to fill 4 inches deep. Heat the oil to 375°.

One by one, remove the oysters from the buttermilk, tapping off excess buttermilk, and dredge in the cornmeal mixture, shaking off excess. Place in the oil to fry, without overcrowding the pan, working in batches as needed. Fry until golden and floating, about 3 minutes. Remove with a slotted spoon to a paper towel lined plate and season with salt and pepper. Continue to fry in batches, each time bringing the oil back to 375° before starting a new batch.

To serve, place a spoonful of the salad in the center of the plate. Top with 5 oysters and drizzle with the mustard sauce.

264

FENNEL-GRAPEFRUIT SALAD

2 large Ruby Red grapefruits
2 bulbs of fennel, tops removed
1 lemon, juiced
¼ cup extra virgin olive oil
Kosher salt and pepper to taste

~

Using a serrated knife, peel the grapefruit, removing the skin and bitter white pith. Cut between the segments to remove the segments, making sure to carefully cut between the bitter membrane. Place the segments in a medium bowl. Once all of the segments are out, squeeze the remaining juice from the membrane into the bowl with the segments.

Using a mandoline, shave the fennel horizontally into paper thin slices. Place the fennel in the bowl with the grapefruit and add the lemon juice and olive oil and gently toss to combine. Season with salt and pepper to taste. Refrigerate until ready to serve.

MAPLE-MUSTARD SAUCE

½ cup dry mustard
½ cup cider vinegar
½ cup granulated sugar
3 large egg yolks
2 tablespoons maple syrup
¼ cup plus 2 tablespoons sour cream

~

In a medium stainless bowl, mix the mustard, vinegar and sugar with a whisk. Whisk in yolks and blend well. Place the bowl over a saucepan of simmering water to form a bain marie. Whisk continuously until thick and the mixture forms ribbons when you lift the whisk. This will take about 5 minutes. Remove the pan from heat and cool. Stir in the maple syrup and fold in the sour cream. Cover and refrigerate until use.

"I'm always learning from books and other cooks. If I don't know how to cook something, I ask if I can cook it with them."

Shrimp Bisque with Bacon Cheddar Crumbs

{ Serves 6 to 8 }

2 pounds fresh Georgia shrimp, head
    and shell on
8 tablespoons unsalted butter, divided
2 Roma tomatoes, diced
1 cup diced yellow onion
1 cup diced celery
½ cup diced carrot
2 bay leaves
4 sprigs fresh parsley

4 sprigs fresh thyme
1 teaspoon crushed red pepper flakes
¼ cup tomato paste
1 tablespoon paprika
¼ cup dry sherry
4 cups milk
1 cup heavy cream
Salt and white pepper to taste
Bacon Cheddar Crumbles

~

Remove the heads and peel and devein the shrimp, saving the heads and tails. Cut the shrimp into bite sized pieces and refrigerate for later use. In a heavy-bottom saucepan, melt 4 tablespoons butter over medium-high heat. Add the shrimp heads and tails and sauté until red, about 5 minutes. Add the diced tomato, onion, celery, carrot, bay leaves, parsley, thyme and red pepper flakes. Reduce the heat to medium and cook until the vegetables are soft and translucent, about 10 minutes. Add the tomato paste and paprika and cook until the mixture starts to caramelize, another 5 minutes or so. Add 2 cups water and bring to a boil. Reduce heat and simmer on low for 1 hour. Remove from the heat.

With an immersion blender, purée the stock (shells and all) and strain through a very fine mesh strainer or cheesecloth, reserving the liquid as the base for the bisque. Return the strained stock to the pan and bring to a boil. Stir the sherry, milk and cream into the base and bring to a boil. Add three-fourths of the shrimp to the bisque and cook for 3 minutes. With an immersion blender, blend the shrimp into the bisque and blend until no pieces remain. Taste and adjust seasonings as needed, with salt and white pepper, and a little cream or sherry to taste. Return the bisque to a boil, and drop in the remaining shrimp, cooking just until curled, another 4 minutes. Serve and top with the bacon cheddar crumbles.

BACON CHEDDAR CRUMBLES

6 strips bacon
½ cup panko (Japanese breadcrumbs)
⅓ cup freshly grated sharp cheddar cheese

~

In a large skillet over medium heat, cook the bacon until crispy. Drain on a paper towel lined plate and cool. Chop the bacon into small bits. Toss the bacon with the panko and cheese and spread on a rimmed baking sheet. Toast until crispy, about 10 minutes.

Heirloom Tomato and Seared Scallop Salad

{ Serves 4 }

1 cup mayonnaise
2 tablespoons finely chopped shallots
1 lemon, juiced
3 tablespoons finely minced dill
Sea salt and freshly ground pepper
4 heirloom tomatoes, rinsed, cores removed
½ cup shaved red onion
3 tablespoons extra virgin olive oil, divided
1 tablespoon high quality balsamic vinegar
12 large fresh diver sea scallops, dry packed
¼ cup high quality bleu cheese, crumbled or grated
12 leaves fresh basil, chiffonade

~

In a small bowl combine the mayonnaise, shallots, lemon juice, dill and 1 teaspoon each salt and pepper. Cover and refrigerate until ready to use.

Slice tomatoes into ½-inch wedges and place in a medium bowl. Gently toss the onion with the tomatoes and sprinkle with salt and pepper. Drizzle with 2 tablespoons olive oil and the balsamic vinegar. Set aside.

Heat a large sauté pan over high heat. Add 1 tablespoon olive oil and heat until hot but not smoking. Season both sides of the scallops with salt and pepper. Place the scallops in the sauté pan without overcrowding. Sear the scallops for 3 minutes per side, until nicely browned and crisp. Drain on a paper towel lined plate.

Divide the tomato mixture between 4 plates. Sprinkle with the bleu cheese. Arrange 3 scallops on each plate and top with a dollop of the herb mayonnaise. Garnish with the basil and serve immediately.

Crispy Grouper with Arugula-Peach Salad and Bourbon-Brown Sugar Vinaigrette

{ Serves 4 }

2 fresh peaches

2 cups arugula

1 small red onion, thinly sliced julienne

1 cup Bourbon-Brown Sugar Vinaigrette, more for garnish

4 5-ounce grouper filets

Kosher salt and freshly ground pepper

1 cup rice flour

Canola oil, for frying

~

Bring a small saucepan of water to a boil. Make an "X" in the blossom end of the peaches and drop in boiling water for 10 seconds. Remove with a slotted spoon and refresh under cold running water. Remove the skin and pit and discard. Slice into ¼-inch thick slices. Place the peaches in a medium bowl. Add arugula and red onion. Set aside.

In a deep sauté pan or deep fat fryer, heat 2 inches of canola oil to 350°. While the oil is heating, season grouper filets with salt and pepper. Dust the filets with the rice flour, shaking off excess. Carefully transfer the grouper filets to the hot oil and fry until golden brown and crisp, approximately 2 minutes per side, or a total of 4 minutes. Remove to a plate lined with paper towels to drain.

To serve, toss the arugula-peach mixture with just enough dressing to coat the leaves, about ⅓ cup. Place a fried grouper filet in the center of the plate and top with the arugula peach salad. Drizzle some of remaining dressing on plate.

BOURBON-BROWN SUGAR VINAIGRETTE

{ Makes 2 cups }

1 small baked sweet potato, peeled

½ cup orange juice

2 tablespoons brown sugar, firmly packed

⅓ cup cider vinegar

½ teaspoon fresh cracked black pepper

Pinch of ground allspice

1 teaspoon kosher salt

¼ cup Kentucky bourbon

½ cup canola oil

1 tablespoon finely chopped shallots

~

Combine in the jar of a blender the peeled sweet potato, orange juice, brown sugar, cider vinegar, pepper, allspice, salt and bourbon. Pulse for 30 seconds to combine. With the blender on, remove the lid and slowly drizzle in the canola oil in a slow steady stream until mixture starts to thicken. Fold in shallots. Season to taste with salt and pepper.

Butterscotch Pudding with Candied Orange Peel and Maple Pecan Sandies

{ Serves 6 to 8 }

2¼ cups whole milk
1 cup heavy cream
1¼ cups brown sugar, firmly packed
6 tablespoons unsalted butter, more for
    the plastic
3 large egg yolks

¼ cup cornstarch
Pinch of fine salt
1 teaspoon vanilla extract
Candied Orange Peel
Maple Pecan Sandies

~

Combine the milk and cream in a medium saucepan over medium-high heat. Bring to a simmer then remove from the heat. In a separate saucepan, combine the brown sugar and butter and cook over medium heat until the sugar is melted. Stir the scalded milk mixture into the brown sugar-butter mixture.

In a medium mixing bowl, combine the egg yolks, cornstarch and salt; whisk together to form a paste. Temper the yolks by adding a little of the milk-sugar mixture to the egg mixture. Then slowly stir the egg mixture into the remaining hot milk-sugar mixture. Cook over medium heat, stirring constantly until the mixture thickens and coats the back of a spoon. Strain the pudding into a medium bowl through a fine mesh sieve. Divide the pudding into individual ramekins. Press buttered plastic wrap or waxed paper directly on the surface of each ramekin to prevent a skin from forming. Refrigerate until cooled and firm, several hours or overnight.

To serve, remove the butterscotch pudding ramekins from the refrigerator and remove the plastic wrap. Top with candied orange peel and serve with the cookies.

CANDIED ORANGE PEEL

1 large or 2 small oranges
2 cups granulated sugar
1 cup water, more for blanching
Pinch of salt

~

With a channel knife or vegetable peeler, peel the oranges, being careful to only remove the skin and none of the bitter white pith. Blanch the skins in a small pot of boiling water. Discard the water and repeat the blanching process two more times, each time using fresh boiling water. Drain, pat dry and set aside.

In a small saucepan combine 1 cup of the granulated sugar and 1 cup of water and bring to a boil to create a simple syrup. Stir the dried, blanched orange peels into the simple syrup and cook over medium heat until thick and syrupy. Using tongs or a slotted spoon, remove the peels and roll in the remaining sugar. Spread the candied peels on a baking sheet and allow to dry, uncovered, overnight.

MAPLE PECAN SANDIES

½ cup pecans, toasted
1 cup all-purpose flour, divided
¼ teaspoon baking powder
Pinch salt
8 tablespoons (1 stick) unsalted butter, room temperature
⅓ cup 10x confectioners' sugar
⅛ teaspoon fine salt
1 teaspoon vanilla extract
½ cup turbinado sugar
2 tablespoons maple syrup

~

Preheat oven to 325°. In the bowl of a food processor fitted with a steel blade, grind the pecans with ½ cup of the flour until it becomes meal. Transfer to a medium bowl. Add remaining ½ cup flour, baking powder and salt. Whisk to combine, set aside.

In the bowl of a stand mixer cream the butter until smooth. Add the powdered sugar and beat until light and fluffy. Add the vanilla and with the mixer on low speed add the flour mixture. Mix until just combined.

With your hands, roll about 1 tablespoon of dough at a time, into balls. Roll in the turbinado sugar and place on a parchment paper lined baking sheet. Press the cookies to flatten slightly. Place in the preheated oven and bake for about ten minutes or until they start to brown around the edges. Remove cookies from the oven and brush with the maple syrup. Transfer cookies to a rack to cool.

WHAT TO DRINK

Seafood has been a major part of cuisines of the world, and not surprisingly wines have been crafted to equal the fruits of the sea. Here are just a few of those wines:

Muscadet Wines from the western Loire Valley based on Chardonnay's cousin, Melon de Bourgogne.

Albariño The Spanish have long been regarded as the world's top fishermen, so it is fitting that we find these wonderful seafood wines there.

Pinot Grigio Seafood would simply not be the same in Venice without Italy's most famous white.

DEAN DUPUIS

became interested in food in his early teens while cooking in pizza joints. By the time he was about 19, Dean decided he was going to focus on a career as a chef which later led him to become executive chef of South City Kitchen in Midtown and Vinings. "I like for people to have fun with their food." He describes his time at the South City Kitchens as "one big ride," which he has enjoyed greatly.

Who are some famous people you've cooked for?
Catherine Zeta-Jones and Michael Douglas, Jimmy Buffett, and Usher. I like to leave the stars alone when they come in.

What are your favorite movies?
Armageddon, Pulp Fiction and *A Few Good Men*.

What would you do if you weren't a chef?
Play professional poker.

What's your favorite book?
On the Trail of the Assassins. It's about the JFK assassination.

What's your favorite drink?
Vodka tonic made with Stoli and extra lime.

What kind of music do you like?
A form of Cuban music that's similar to American rap, and I like Steely Dan.

What would you do if you won the lottery?
I'd buy a small restaurant that served dinner only. It would be closed two days a week so I could take a break.

What's your favorite kitchen tool?
I bought a Microplane five years ago and I can't put it down.

If you could cook for anyone, who would it be?
James Beard, the "Father of American Cooking."

Aria www.aria-atl.com
490 East Paces Ferry Road – Atlanta, GA 30305 **404-233-7673**

Bold American Catering www.fifthgroup.com
887 West Marietta Street, Studio K-102 – Atlanta, GA 30318 **404-815-1178**

Canoe www.canoeatl.com
4199 Paces Ferry Road – Atlanta, GA 30339 **770-432-2663**

Catering 101 www.101concepts.com
5229 Roswell Road – Atlanta, GA 30342 **404-250-0947**

Dish www.dish-atlanta.com
870 North Highland Avenue – Atlanta, GA 30306 **404-897-3463**

Ecco www.fifthgroup.com
40 7th Street – Atlanta, GA 30308 **404-347-9555**

Einstein's www.einsteinsatlanta.com
1077 Juniper Street – Atlanta, GA 30309 **404-876-7925**

Food 101 www.101concepts.com
Sandy Springs – 4969 Roswell Road, Suite 200 – Sandy Springs, GA 30342 **404-497-9700**
Morningside – 1397 North Highland Avenue – Atlanta, GA 30306 **404-347-9747**

The Food Studio www.fifthgroup.com
887 West Marietta Street – Atlanta, GA 30318 **404-815-6677**

Garrison's Broiler & Tap www.garrisonsatlanta.com
Vinings – 4300 Paces Ferry Road – Atlanta, GA 30339 **770-436-0102**
Perimeter – 4400 Ashford Dunwoody Road – Atlanta, GA 30346 **770-350-0134**
Duluth – 9700 Medlock Bridge Road – Duluth, GA 30097 **770-476-1962**

The Globe www.globeatlanta.com
75 Fifth Street – Atlanta, GA 30308 **404-541-1487**

Joël www.joelrestaurant.com
3290 Northside Parkway – Atlanta, GA 30327 **404-233-3500**

La Tavola Trattoria www.fifthgroup.com
992 Virginia Avenue – Atlanta, GA 30306 **404-873-5430**

Lobby at Twelve www.lobbyattwelve.com
361 17th Street – Atlanta, GA 30363 **404-961-7370**

Meehan's Public House www.101concepts.com
Sandy Springs – 227 Sandy Springs Place, Suite 416 – Sandy Springs, GA 30328 **404-843-8058**
Vinings – 2810 Paces Ferry Road, Suite 300 – Atlanta, GA 30339 **770-433-1920**
Brookhaven – 4058 Peachtree Road, Suite C – Atlanta, GA 30319 **404-467-9531**
Alpharetta – 11130 Statebridge Road – Alpharetta, GA 30022 **770-475-2468**

Metrotainment Bakery www.metrobakery.com
691 14th Street – Atlanta, GA 30309 **404-873-6307**

Pangaea
1082 Huff Road – Atlanta, GA 30318 **404-350-8787**

Pricci buckheadrestaurants.com
500 Pharr Road – Atlanta, GA 30305 **404-237-2941**

Rainwater www.rainwaterrestaurant.com
11655 Haynes Bridge Road – Alpharetta, GA 30004 **770-777-0033**

Rathbun's www.rathbunsrestaurant.com
112 Krog Street, Suite R – Atlanta, Georgia 30307 **404-524-8280**

Sala – Sabor de Mexico www.fifthgroup.com
1186 North Highland Avenue – Atlanta, GA 30306 **404-872-7203**

Shaun's
1029 Edgewood Avenue – Atlanta, GA 30307 **404-577-4358**

SoHo www.sohoatlanta.com
4300 Paces Ferry Road – Atlanta, GA 30339 **770-801-0069**

South City Kitchen www.fifthgroup.com
Vinings – 1675 Cumberland Parkway – Smyrna, GA 30080 **770-435-0700**
Midtown – 1144 Crescent Avenue – Atlanta, GA 30309 **404-873-7358**

Via Elisa Fresh Pasta www.viaelisa.com
1750 Howell Mill Road – Atlanta, GA 30318 **404-605-0668**

Virginia Willis www.virginiawillis.com

Watershed www.watershedrestaurant.com
406 West Ponce De Leon Avenue – Decatur, GA 30030 **404-378-4900**

Wisteria www.wisteria-atlanta.com
471 North Highlands Boulevard – Atlanta, GA 30307 **404-525-3363**

Woodfire Grill www.woodfiregrill.com
1782 Cheshire Bridge Road – Atlanta, GA 30324 **404-347-9055**

al denté: An Italian phrase meaning "to the tooth," usually used when describing pasta or other food that is cooked just until it offers a slight resistance when bitten into, but is not soft or overdone.

bain marie: French for water bath. It consists of placing a container of food in a large, shallow pan of warm water, surrounding the food with gentle heat. Food may be cooked this way in an oven or on top of a range. Chefs use this technique to cook delicate dishes such as custards, sauces and savory mousses without breaking or curdling them, or just to keep cooked foods warm.

blanch: To plunge food into boiling water briefly, then into cold water to stop the cooking process. This firms the flesh, loosens the skin, and heightens and sets color and flavor.

caramelize: The process in which foods are heated and the natural sugars turn brown.

celery root: Also called celeriac and celery knob, this knobby, brown vegetable is cultivated specifically for its root. It tastes like a mix between celery and parsley. Growing season is September through May.

chiffonade: A classic French cut, fine strips or shreds. This cut is usually used on tender greens.

deglaze: After a food has been sautéed and all removed from the pan, you deglaze the pan by adding a small amount of liquid to the pan and stirring to loosen the browned bits of food on the bottom of the pan, creating a base for a sauce or glaze.

emulsion, emulsify: A mixture of one liquid with another which do not normally combine smoothly such as oil and water. To emulsify, you very slowly add one ingredient to another while at the same time mixing rapidly, dispersing and suspending minute droplets of one liquid throughout the other. Emulsified mixtures are usually thick and satiny.

fingerling: An heirloom variety of potato that is small and brown, about the size of your thumb.

fleur de sel: Literally translated means "flowers of the sea," referring to artisan or hand-harvested sea salt.

French, to: 1. To cut a vegetable or meat lengthwise into very thin strips. Beans and potatoes are commonly "frenched." 2. To cut the meat away from the end of a rib or chop, exposing part of the bone.

gastrique: French for "gastric," referring to a syrupy reduction of caramelized sugar and vinegar typically used in savory dishes that include fruit, such as oranges or tomatoes.

ice bath: A mixture of ice and cold water used to "shock" or stop cooking. To blanch vegetables, remove from the boiling water and immediately plunge into a large bowl of ice and water (ice bath) to instantly stop the cooking process. Can also be used to crisp vegetables such as celery or lettuce.

involtini: Thin slices of meat, fish or vegetables stuffed and rolled. Typically they are then grilled, baked or sautéed.

julienne: A classic French cut, a thin matchstick strip ⅛-inch x ⅛-inch, any length desired.

muddle: To mash or crush ingredients with a spoon or a muddler (a rod with a flattened end). Used with the preparation of mixed drinks, such as when mint leaves and sugar are muddled together for a mint julep.

non-reactive saucepan: A stainless steel saucepan that does not cause ingredients to have an adverse effect with the pan they are cooked in. Cast iron and aluminum tend to react, in general terms, to acidic (tomatoes) and sulfuric compounds (eggs) forming an undesirable change in color or flavor.

reduce: To boil a liquid rapidly until the volume is reduced by evaporation, thickening the consistency and intensifying the flavor.

render: To melt animal fat over low heat separating it from any connective pieces of tissue, which will turn brown and crisp and are generally referred to as cracklings.

saba: A by-product of balsamic vinegar, it's a slightly sweet, unfermented syrup made from the must of Trebbiano grapes. It can be found in specialty food stores such as Whole Foods, near the vinegar.

score: To make shallow cuts in the surface of certain foods, such as meat or fish. This is done to decorate some foods (breads and meats), to assist flavor absorption (as with marinated foods), to tenderize less tender cuts of meat, and to allow excess fat to drain during cooking.

shock: To stop the cooking process, such as when blanching vegetables.

Silpat: Brand of non-stick silicone baking sheet.

sweat: A technique by which ingredients are cooked in a small amount of fat over low heat so they soften without browning, and cook in their own juices. Commonly used with vegetables.

turbinado sugar: Raw sugar that has been steam-cleaned. Turbinado crystals are coarse, blond colored, and have a delicate molasses flavor.

yuzu: A sour Japanese citrus fruit used almost exclusively for its aromatic rind.

zest: The outer skin layer of citrus which contains the flavorful oils used to add citrus flavor without the acidic juice. Use a microplane grater for zesting (fine shreds). Sometimes long strips of zest are used for garnish.